Contents

✳

Commissioned

One day during my second bout with cancer, my wife was rubbing my back to relieve the tension from the dry heaves when *she* walked in my hospital room, just as perky as ever. A teacher in Christian schools for 25 years, people say, "It makes a difference if your child can have *her* as a teacher."

During the visit, she touched on the need for devotions for Christian teachers. After a thoughtful pause, she looked at me and said, "You should write some." She snapped her fingers and smiled, "I now commission you to write for Christian teachers." I laughed. Later, when I was alone, I began to think about her visit. I decided to take her commissioning seriously.

When cancer strikes the second time, you begin to wonder how much time you have left. But our "Job" experiences aren't meant to produce only an "Ah, poor me!" attitude. In fact, God uses every experience, good or bad, to draw us closer to Him. That day I told God that my life was in His hands, no matter what happened, and that I did not consider the words "I commission you" to be accidental or idle. On the wall of my hospital room hung a large calendar, the kind with one day per page. It showed November 3. I got out of bed, ripped off the page, and stuck it in my travel bag. I wanted to remember.

As a Christian teacher you are commissioned by God. What a unique experience! Your commissioning began with the faith, abilities, and experiences God sent into your life. He trained you and set you apart for your special calling. The authority of your commission lies in the great

"Go, therefore!" of Jesus. You are appointed to be the mouth and hands of Christ to your students. Your work is classified as active service. The message you are to speak has been clearly spelled out in the Scriptures. The Commissioning Officer has great expectations of you, but He will also be the one to uphold you and encourage you.

God's Words of Encouragement

Be strong and courageous. Do not be terrified; do not be discouraged, for the LORD your God will be with you wherever you go. *Joshua 1:9*

Show me Your ways, O LORD, teach me Your paths; guide me in Your truth and teach me, for You are God my Savior, and my hope is in You all day long. *Psalm 25:4–5*

I will instruct you and teach you in the way you should go; I will counsel you and watch over you. *Psalm 32:8*

I urge you to live a life worthy of the calling you have received. Be completely humble and gentle; be patient, bearing with one another in love. Make every effort to keep the unity of the Spirit through the bond of peace. *Ephesians 4:1–3*

Live a life worthy of the Lord and … please Him in every way: bearing fruit in every good work, growing in the knowledge of God, being strengthened with all power according to His glorious might so that you may have great endurance and patience, and joyfully giving thanks to the Father, who has qualified you to share in the inheritance of the saints in the kingdom of light. *Colossians 1:10–12*

If anyone speaks, he should do it as one speaking the very words of God. If anyone serves, he should do it with the strength God provides, so that in all things God may be praised through Jesus Christ. *1 Peter 4:11*

✳

A Wonderful Opportunity

My wife and I waited five years to adopt Bradley. Then we went to Africa. Bradley died there at age five from a fever that had also taken the life of one of his friends.

I stayed in the hospital for a month with Bradley. I watched the rigors of the periodic high fevers, slowly take their toll on his body. When the fevers would suddenly shoot up to 105° and 106°, the doctors would pack Bradley in ice the missionaries in the area supplied.

One January morning, Bradley said to me, "Don't let them put me in ice because Jesus is coming today." I looked at him quietly and touched his shoulder without saying a word. At 7:30 that evening, a nurse took his vitals and said, "Your son is dying." I put my head next to the oxygen tent and heard Bradley say in a heavy whisper, "Jesus is coming now." In a few moments, Jesus did come.

Why tell you about this? Because someone had a wonderful opportunity to raise Bradley as God's child. I credit his mother for much of this. She never let a day end without talking to Bradley about God, telling him Bible stories, and praying with him. Oh, I taught him too, but I wasn't always there. Because of my wife's diligent instruction, God became a wonderful personal friend of Bradley's. God helped Bradley in his final illness, and Jesus took Bradley to be with Him in heaven.

You have the same wonderful opportunity and responsibility to educate the children in your class about

God. As a teacher, be willing to share your faith. Let children see and hear what Jesus means to you. Take time to talk plainly about your relationship with God. Let children hear you pray in the classroom. Allow children to express their faith and let them lead prayers. Make devotions a highlight in your classroom. Use God's Word to set the mood and feeling for the day, and then give your students the opportunity to express that spirit throughout the day.

Though you will never hear it, some day your former students, led by God's Holy Spirit, may confidently say, "Jesus is coming now."

God's Words of Encouragement

May the favor of the Lord our God rest upon us; establish the work of our hands for us—yes, establish the work of our hands. *Psalm 90:17*

Praise the LORD, O my soul, and forget not all His benefits—who forgives all your sins and heals all your diseases, who redeems your life from the pit and crowns you with love and compassion, who satisfies your desires with good things so that your youth is renewed like the eagle's. *Psalm 103:2–5*

It was good for me to be afflicted so that I might learn Your decrees. *Psalm 119:71*

The LORD will keep you from all harm—He will watch over your life; the LORD will watch over your coming and going both now and forevermore. *Psalm 121:7–8*

Each one should use whatever gift he has received to serve others, faithfully administering God's grace in its various forms. *1 Peter 4:10*

Only hold on to what you have until I come. *Revelation 2:25*

"Let us rejoice and be glad and give Him glory! For the wedding of the Lamb has come, and His bride has made herself ready. Fine linen, bright and clean, was given her to wear." … "Blessed are those who are invited to the wedding supper of the Lamb!" *Revelation 19:7–9*

He who testifies to these things says, "Yes, I am coming soon." Amen. Come, Lord Jesus. *Revelation 22:20*

God Is Great, God Is Good

When I was in eighth-grade confirmation class, my pastor emphasized how important it was to really know God. A section of Martin Luther's Small Catechism lists the attributes of God. I wrote this prayer to help me realize how God's attributes reveal His greatness and how each attribute affects my life. This prayer praises God for His presence in my life as a personal friend.

A Prayer

Dear heavenly Father, You are the great *eternal* God. You are not a creature of time as I am. I live the past, present, and future of my life knowing I'm part of Your eternal plan. Through my Lord Jesus Christ, I have the hope of an eternal heaven.

Gracious God, You are the *unchangeable* God. My moods, my trust can vary from time to time, but while I have changed, You have not. Each of Your holy attributes remains the same, and I have every reason to trust Your unchangeableness.

Almighty God, You are the great *omnipotent* One. All things are possible through Your almighty power. I regret that too often my mistrust hinders Your omnipotence. In Your almighty power, You have set the order of the universe and the order of my life. You uphold all that You have made.

Great all-knowing God, You are the *omniscient* One. Nothing can be hidden from You and no one can deceive You. Because You are omniscient, help me deal honestly with You and those around me.

Heavenly Father, as the *omnipresent* One, You fill heaven and earth. No one can hide from You. Your omnipresence comforts me because I know that You are by the side of those I pray for, just as You are with me. Thank You for Your omnipresence, which makes You my personal friend and God.

Great God, You are *holy and just.* Your holiness and justice set the absolutes for faltering, sinful humanity. Curb my willfulness and fickleness, which oppose Your holiness.

Heavenly Father, You are *faithful and benevolent.* You keep Your promises. Thank You for overcoming evil in this world through Your Son's obedient life, death, and resurrection. Though I live in an evil world, I believe in Your promise that You will destroy this world and take me and all believers to be with You in heaven.

God, You are *merciful and gracious.* Out of Your abundant goodness, You offer forgiveness for the world's iniquities. Lord, grant me faith to see Your mercy and grace at work in my life.

Great God, You are the *sovereign* One. Your sovereignty demands my submission. As the sovereign God, You do whatever You wish, to whomever You wish. If You were only a *jealous* God, Your sovereignty would be something to fear, but You are also a God of unconditional *love.* You only do what is good for me, whether in blessing or in discipline.

Indeed, You are the great and good God. You invest Yourself in the care of Your creation and all Your attributes are a blessing to me.

God's Words of Encouragement

When I consider Your heavens, the work of Your fingers,

the moon and the stars, which You have set in place, what is man that You are mindful of him, the son of man that You care for him? You made him a little lower than the heavenly beings and crowned him with glory and honor. *Psalm 8:3–5*

Ascribe to the LORD the glory due His name; worship the LORD in the splendor of His holiness. *Psalm 29:2*

You remain the same, and Your years will never end. *Psalm 102:27*

You will keep in perfect peace him whose mind is steadfast, because he trusts in You. Trust in the LORD forever, for the LORD, the LORD, is the Rock eternal. *Isaiah 26:3–4*

This is the one I esteem: he who is humble and contrite in spirit, and trembles at My word. *Isaiah 66:2*

May God Himself, the God of peace, sanctify you through and through. May your whole spirit, soul and body be kept blameless at the coming of our Lord Jesus Christ. The one who calls you is faithful and He will do it. *1 Thessalonians 5:23–24*

You are worthy, our Lord and God, to receive glory and honor and power, for You created all things, and by Your will they were created and have their being. *Revelation 4:11*

❋

What Does This Mean?

When you read Martin Luther's Small Catechism, you get the impression that he liked the question, "What does this mean?" I wonder if he realized how his explanations provide a list of seven things we owe to God?

In the explanation to the First Commandment, Luther writes: "We should fear, love, and trust in God above all things." In the explanation to the Second Article of the Apostles' Creed, Luther writes: "For all which it is my duty to thank, praise, serve, and obey Him." According to Luther, these are the seven ways we respond to God: fear, love, trust, thank, praise, serve, and obey.

Fear God. Stand in awe of God's perfection. Don't put Him in a box. He has the power to handle every situation.

Love God. The Bible says to love God with all your heart, soul, and mind—that is, with all your being. It's easy to give God a selfish love based on what you have received. But the love God's Holy Spirit plants in your heart stems from all that God has done for you in Jesus. His love is unconditional.

Trust God. Trusting God at all times can be a challenge—an impossibility without the Holy Spirit's leading. A strong will and personal opinions can take precedence. But you can trust God completely because He always has your welfare at heart. He delights in being your heavenly Father. Trust in God; submit your will to His plan for your life.

Praise and thank God. God responds to you. He hears the praise and thanks of His people.

Serve God. God walks with you. He offers you all His blessings, and in turn, you are blessed and saved to serve

Him. A good relationship involves receiving and responding. You receive salvation and respond with service to God.

Obey God. When Jesus died for the sins of the world, He did not remove the command to obey God. While it's true that obedience doesn't save you, you do show your love for God through obedience.

God's Words of Encouragement

But as for me, it is good to be near God. I have made the Sovereign LORD my refuge; I will tell of all Your deeds. *Psalm 73:28*

The LORD takes delight in His people; He crowns the humble with salvation. Let the saints rejoice in this honor and sing for joy on their beds. *Psalm 149:4–5*

You yourselves are our letter, written on our hearts, known and read by everybody. You show that you are a letter from Christ, the result of our ministry, written not with ink but with the Spirit of the living God, not on tablets of stone but on tablets of human hearts. *2 Corinthians 3:2*

And as for you, brothers, never tire of doing what is right. *2 Thessalonians 3:13*

Therefore, rid yourselves of all malice and all deceit, hypocrisy, envy, and slander of every kind. Like newborn babies, crave pure spiritual milk, so that by it you may grow up in your salvation, now that you have tasted that the Lord is good. *1 Peter 2:1–3*

This is how we know that we love the children of God: by loving God and carrying out His commands. This is love for God: to obey His commands. And His commands are not burdensome. *1 John 5:2–3*

*

When God Covers My Face

Exodus 33 always intrigues me. Here Moses challenged God's promise to be with him. Moses asked God to show him His glory. God told Moses that His glory will pass before him, but Moses cannot see God's face. Moses hid in the cleft of a rock, God passed by, and He placed His hand over Moses' face. God said, "You will see My back, but My face must not be seen."

God covers my face at times too. I can't see the plans God has for me. But I do see God's back. I know the multitude of ways God has worked in my past. Because I know what God has done for me, I can trust Him for the future.

Exodus 33 clearly shows God's great wisdom as He deals with His unpredictable human creatures. How would I, as a sinner, act if God would let me see His face, see all His plans for me? Would I argue, throw tantrums, make every effort to show that I am wiser than God? Knowing my future would lessen my trust in God. I would no longer depend on His great wisdom. His great glory would carry little meaning. What unimaginable confusion would reign if God allowed me to see His face, His plans for my future.

As a Christian teacher, you also might wish to see God's face so that you could put some of your concerns to rest. But God says, "Trust Me." Trust can be difficult, especially when life includes unexpected events for which you are ill-prepared. God has your best interests at heart.

He works through all things for your good. You can rely on this promise.

God's Words of Encouragement

But I trust in You, O Lord; I say, "You are my God." My times are in Your hands; deliver me from my enemies and from those who pursue me. Let Your face shine on Your servant; save me in Your unfailing love. *Psalm 31:14–16*

Teach us to number our days aright, that we may gain a heart of wisdom. May Your deeds be shown to Your servants, Your splendor to their children. *Psalm 90:12, 16*

Unless the Lord had given me help, I would soon have dwelt in the silence of death. When I said, "My foot is slipping," Your love, O Lord, supported me. When anxiety was great within me, Your consolation brought joy to my soul. *Psalm 94:17–19*

Now listen, you who say, "Today or tomorrow we will go to this or that city, spend a year there, carry on business and make money." Why, you do not even know what will happen tomorrow. What is your life? You are a mist that appears for a little while and then vanishes. Instead, you ought to say, "If it is the Lord's will, we will live and do this or that." As it is, you boast and brag. All such boasting is evil. Anyone, then, who knows the good he ought to do and doesn't do it, sins. *James 4:13–17*

Create a Right Spirit within Me

Sometimes I don't like how I feel. I can't quite put my finger on it, but God seems far away. Frustrations stalk me, and my heart carries a burden of anger. I complain easily. I feel sorry for myself.

I've tried to get back in the swing of things, get myself under control, but I can't bounce back. A spiritual tiredness plagues my heart, and my emotions overwhelm me. I lose my perspective on life, and sometimes I'm not sure that I even care.

How can this happen to me—a child of God? How can this happen to someone who claims to love God? God seems to have emptied my cup, and I don't understand why He won't fill it back up.

Spiritual loneliness plagued even God's chosen representatives. Elijah got so spiritually disheartened that he asked God to take him home to heaven. Job accepted but didn't understand the afflictions God allowed in his life.

God doesn't abandon us to our problems. He travels with us, even to the depths of despair. He holds our hand as we fall on our knees and cry, "Lord, I can't make it on my own. Create in me a clean heart, O God, and renew a right spirit within me." Then God sends His Spirit to minister to us and restore us.

The Holy Spirit eagerly waits to minister to you. Ask God to focus your life and your faith on Christ, your Savior and Lord. God's grace and providence will restore you. Trust Him to direct you along His paths. Be still and know that He is God. He is willing to fill your empty cup with His Holy Spirit.

God's Words of Encouragement

Wait for the LORD; be strong and take heart and wait for the LORD. *Psalm 27:14*

Then I acknowledged my sin to You and did not cover up my iniquity. I said, "I will confess my transgressions to the LORD"—and You forgave the guilt of my sin. Therefore let everyone who is godly pray to You while You may be found; surely when the mighty waters rise, they will not reach him. You are my hiding place; You will protect me from trouble and surround me with songs of deliverance. *Psalm 32:5–7*

Create in me a pure heart, O God, and renew a steadfast spirit within me. Do not cast me from Your presence or take Your Holy Spirit from me. *Psalm 51:10–11*

As water reflects a face, so a man's heart reflects the man. *Proverbs 27:19*

He who conceals his sins does not prosper, but whoever confesses and renounces them finds mercy. *Proverbs 28:13*

Finally, brothers, whatever is true, whatever is noble, whatever is right, whatever is pure, whatever is lovely, whatever is admirable—if anything is excellent or praiseworthy—think about such things. *Philippians 4:8*

My Hip Is Out of Place

In Genesis 32, Jacob was preparing to meet his brother, Esau, for the first time in 20 years. Jacob had every reason to be afraid. At their last meeting, Jacob had stolen Esau's birthright. The coming event was fraught with danger. Jacob needed to know God would be with him during the meeting. Jacob struggled with his emotions and with God all night.

Few Christians escape such a personal struggle. It happens to teachers too. The struggle may involve death, a serious illness, the consideration of a new position, taking responsibility for a careless act, facing someone's anger, or facing discouragement. Struggling with God through these situations may leave a lasting reminder, like a hip that is out of place.

But our almighty God does respond to the fervent prayers of His children. When you call out, "God hear my prayer. I will not let You go unless You answer me with Your blessing," He will respond. Beyond anything we can comprehend, God's great power touches us in unexpected ways to remind us of the power of prayer.

Jacob probably never forgot the night he was alone with God. Exhausted from wrestling, all Jacob could do was cling to his opponent. But he wouldn't let go, and he demanded a blessing. God granted his request and changed his name to Israel because he had struggled with God and with men and had overcome. Jacob called the place *Peniel* because he had "seen God face to face." Jacob limped away with a hip out of place to remind him of his struggle with God.

Such fervent struggles are not easily forgotten. Answered prayers should not be overlooked either. God uses both to make lasting and sometimes life-changing impressions. What has God knocked out of place in your life?

God's Words of Encouragement

Hear my voice when I call, O Lᴏʀᴅ; be merciful to me and answer me. My heart says of You, "See His face!" Your face, Lᴏʀᴅ, I will seek. Do not hide Your face from me, do not turn Your servant away in anger; You have been my helper. Do not reject me or forsake me, O God my Savior. *Psalm 27:7–9*

[Jesus said,] "Do not let your hearts be troubled. Trust in God, trust also in Me." *John 14:1*

[Jesus said,] "Peace I leave with you; My peace I give you. I do not give to you as the world gives. Do not let your hearts be troubled and do not be afraid." *John 14:27*

But thanks be to God! He gives us the victory through our Lord Jesus Christ. *1 Corinthians 15:57*

As God has said: "I will live with them and walk among them, and I will be their God, and they will be My people." *2 Corinthians 6:16*

Who is it that overcomes the world? Only he who believes that Jesus is the Son of God. *1 John 5:5*

This is the confidence we have in approaching God: that if we ask anything according to His will, He hears us. *1 John 5:14*

He who overcomes will, like them, be dressed in white. I will never blot out his name from the book of life, but will acknowledge his name before My Father and His angels. *Revelation 3:5*

To him who overcomes, I will give the right to sit with Me on My throne, just as I overcame and sat down with My Father on His throne. *Revelation 3:21*

*

In Grandstand Number 1— Abraham

Sports fans and athletes know the importance of the cheering section. A loyal audience encourages its team whether it is winning or losing.

Players in the game of life also need a cheering section. Imagine Grandstand Number 1 with one person in it, cheering you on. You know him from the Bible. His name is Abraham. Listen to his words of support to you as a teacher.

"You teach in a world much different but also very similar to my first homeland, Ur, and to the country God led me to, Canaan. Like you, I left my family to go to a place I did not know. I remember feeling insecure, but God continually reminded me of His promises. The same God keeps His promises to you. Trust Him always in all things.

"One day God said to me, 'I will bless you so that you may be a blessing to others.' And God kept His promise because He sent His Son, Jesus, to earth through my descendants. And through Jesus, God kept His promise to send a Savior to the world. You also are a blessing to others. As you read God's Word and teach about His actions, the Holy Spirit works in your students' hearts. In this way, God uses you to spread His saving message and to be a blessing to others.

"Your God is devoted to you. He claims you as His

child. I wish I could explain how much God loves you, but only when He takes you to Himself in heaven will you fully understand His love for you.

"Ask God to strengthen your trust in Him. I waited many years for the answers to my prayers. I learned that God's timing is much better than mine. Even though I sometimes felt like giving up, God reminded me that He was faithful to His promises.

"I hope you find satisfaction in your calling. Teaching will not be without its difficult moments, but God will use each experience to mold you into a better teacher. I'll be cheering you on because like you, I am one of God's chosen ones, set apart that God's will might be accomplished."

God's Words of Encouragement

The LORD had said to Abram, "Leave your country, your people and your father's household and go to the land I will show you. I will make you into a great nation and I will bless you; I will make your name great, and you will be a blessing." *Genesis 12:1–2*

Abram believed the LORD, and He credited it to him as righteousness. *Genesis 15:6*

Glorify the LORD with me; let us exalt His name together. I sought the LORD, and He answered me; He delivered me from all my fears. Those who look to Him are radiant; their faces are never covered with shame. *Psalm 34:3–5*

I have fought the good fight, I have finished the race, I have kept the faith. Now there is in store for me the crown of righteousness, which the Lord, the righteous

Judge, will award to me on that day—and not only to me, but also to all who have longed for His appearing. *2 Timothy 4:7–8*

You see that [Abraham's] faith and his actions were working together, and his faith was made complete by what he did. And the scripture was fulfilled that says, "Abraham believed God, and it was credited to him as righteousness." *James 2:22–23*

*

In Grandstand Number 2—Moses

Another of God's saints cheers you on from Grandstand Number 2. Moses, one of God's chosen leaders, appeared with Jesus at His transfiguration. His presence helped cheer the three disciples present at this miracle, and Moses has some words of advice and encouragement for you as well.

"As a person ministering to God's people, you should expect two things. One is a lot of work, and the other is great blessings from God. If I had fully understood all that God expected of me when He spoke to me from the burning bush, I would have had even more doubts. But had I not followed God's call, I would not have experienced His mighty power and mercy.

"As a Christian teacher, carefully look for the ways God guides your life and sends His goodness to you every day. Stand in awe of His providence. I was 80 years old when God called me to lead His people out of bondage to the Promised Land. But I can see as I look back how God prepared me for this role. As a child, my mother taught me about God. As the adopted son of an Egyptian princess, I was given the best education. I learned the Egyptian language and culture. As a fugitive, I fled to the desert of Midian and became a shepherd. In these very different experiences, God worked to mold me into the leader of His people Israel. When you wonder where God is taking you, be patient and submit to His will. He is fitting you into His plan.

"The experience of the burning bush remains vivid in my mind. In awe I watched a bush that seemed to be burning and yet was not destroyed. Then I heard God's voice telling me I was standing on holy ground. You will have similar experiences. At times God's directives will be so clear and challenging that your heart will tremble. You will find yourself being set apart. You may be afraid and unsure, but God will protect you and provide the answers to your questions.

"As a Christian teacher, you will experience the gamut of feelings, just as I did. I often felt caught between the people's complaints and God's anger. It could be so frustrating. I experienced fear as I stood before Pharaoh; disgust when the people complained about the manna; anger when I saw the golden calf; joy when I heard the people repent and God declare His forgiveness; love for a God whose mercy had no end; awe at the sound of God's voice; arrogance when I said, 'must we fetch you water'; humility as I begged for forgiveness for myself; numbness when God said we would wander in the desert for 40 years. Do these same emotions overwhelm you at times? These too shall pass. A Mount Nebo awaits you, as well, where the Lord Himself will give you your reward.

"So I chcei you on in the words God spoke to Joshua, the man He chose to follow me: 'Be strong and courageous.' "

God's Words of Encouragement

"Do not come any closer," God said. "Take off your sandals, for the place where you are standing is holy ground. ... So now, go. I am sending you." *Exodus 3:5, 10*

25

The LORD gives strength to His people; the LORD blesses His people with peace. *Psalm 29:11*

See, I have engraved you on the palms of My hands. *Isaiah 49:16*

I will tell of the kindnesses of the LORD, the deeds for which He is to be praised, according to all the LORD has done for us—yes, the many good things He has done for the house of Israel, according to His compassion and many kindnesses. … In all their distress He too was distressed, and the angel of His presence saved them. In His love and mercy He redeemed them; He lifted them up and carried them all the days of old. *Isaiah 63:7, 9*

In Grandstand Number 3—Paul

Another biblical cheerleader offers his support from Grandstand Number 3—the apostle Paul.

"My life is an absolute miracle. I was one of God's greatest enemies. Oh, I knew Him, even stood in awe of Him. I knew the scriptures from A to Z because I had been taught by the best. I was devoted to God's cause, or at least what I thought was His cause.

"And then the light of Jesus Christ struck me down on the way to Damascus! I lay there in the light, accused, convicted. God changed me forever. He directed me to people who protected and befriended me. Ananias baptized me. Others instructed me in my new faith. God made me one of His special friends. My life illustrates that with God all things are possible.

"I don't know where you are in your faith or life, but I do know that God will change you and direct you for His purposes. You can easily mess up your ministry when you do what *you* think is right without asking God what He wants. You too may have a Damascus experience. Jesus may challenge you to turn the direction of your life upside down.

"How different my life was after God made me a Christian. I worked with wonderful people like Barnabas and Timothy. Together, God used us to spread the salvation message, not just to our own people but to the pagan world. I no longer tried to imprison Christians, but God used me to reach people for Him and to encourage Christians in their faith. Isn't this also your job as a Christian teacher? You teach the lambs about their Savior, Jesus Christ. What an awesome responsibility.

"Your ministry will not be a bed of roses. You will find joy in what you do rather than in experiencing a life free of difficulties. My life had its problems—beatings, a shipwreck, a thorn in the flesh, and several imprisonments. Because we want an easy life, it's easy to fall into self-pity when things go wrong. But count these trials as benefits because God will work through them to strengthen you and provide a witness of your faith to those around you. Keep your eyes on Jesus, and your joy will be complete.

"I'm proud that you have chosen to be a Christian teacher. Count each day as an opportunity to serve your Lord. Glorify and praise Him in all you do."

God's Words of Encouragement

Be strong and take heart, all you who hope in the LORD. *Psalm 31:24*

For it is commendable if a man bears up under the pain of unjust suffering because he is conscious of God. *1 Peter 2:19*

For this very reason, make every effort to add to your faith goodness; and to goodness, knowledge; and to knowledge, self-control; and to self-control, perseverance; and to perseverance, godliness; and to godliness, brotherly kindness; and to brotherly kindness, love. For if you possess these qualities in increasing measure, they will keep you from being ineffective and unproductive in your knowledge of our Lord Jesus Christ. *2 Peter 1:5–8*

We know that we live in Him and He in us, because He

has given us of His Spirit. And we have seen and testify that the Father has sent His Son to be the Savior of the world. If anyone acknowledges that Jesus is the Son of God, God lives in him and he in God. And so we know and rely on the love God has for us. *1 John 4:13–16*

To those who have been called, who are loved by God the Father and kept by Jesus Christ. … Dear friends, although I was very eager to write to you about the salvation we share, I felt I had to write and urge you to contend for the faith that was once for all entrusted to the saints. *Jude 1:1, 3*

✳

Gems from Deuteronomy

It's my understanding that because Muslims believe their Koran is a holy book, they cannot mark in it. I would make a poor Muslim. While I admire such respect, the pages of my Bible are covered with notes. Especially the book of Deuteronomy. Here are some of Deuteronomy's gems.

- *"The LORD your God, who is going before you, will fight for you" (Deuteronomy 1:30).* Because God goes before you, you don't have to worry about anything, not even the first day of school. A prepared teacher who turns the day over to God will not be disappointed. Read that sentence again, all you beginning teachers!

- *What other nation is so great as to have their gods near them the way the LORD our God is near us whenever we pray to Him? (Deuteronomy 4:7).* What could be better than to be near a God who loves you unconditionally? Turn all your worries over to Him and share all your joys with the God who loves you.

- *Love the LORD your God with all your heart and with all your soul and with all your strength (Deuteronomy 6:5).* God's love for you is so great that He sent His Son, Jesus, to die for you. His Spirit motivates you to return this love in all you do and say.

- *"In the future, when your son asks you, 'What is the meaning of the stipulations, decrees and laws the LORD our God has commanded you?' tell him: …" (Deuteronomy 6:20).* As a Christian teacher, you have the oppor-

30

tunity and mandate to share the Word of God with your students. This includes sharing the Gospel message as well as God's commands for how we are to live our lives.

- *When you have eaten and are satisfied, praise the LORD your God for the good land He has given you. Be careful that you do not forget the LORD your God (Deuteronomy 8:10–11).* If you become too self-confident, if your schedule becomes too hectic, if your priorities become confused, you easily can forget God. Daily ask Him to guide your decisions and move you along the path He has set before you.

- *Deuteronomy 28.* This chapter lists two choices in life, choices for blessings or choices for curses. Young Christians need to understand the truths of this chapter. God will bless those who, in faith, express their love and obedience. Those who do not believe and turn away from God will suffer eternally for their disobedience.

- *Your strength will equal your days (Deuteronomy 33:25).* Take comfort in the fact that God knows the needs of each hectic day, and He gives you strength accordingly. Recognize God's many gifts of help and support and thank Him for them.

- *The eternal God is your refuge, and underneath are the everlasting arms. (Deuteronomy 33:27).* God's arms always support you. They are there to hold you up, guide you, and protect you.

- *Blessed are you, O Israel! Who is like you, a people saved by the LORD? (Deuteronomy 33:29).* Rejoice in God's daily care and praise Him for His gift of salvation through His Son, Jesus Christ.

- *Since then, no prophet has risen in Israel like Moses, whom the LORD knew face to face (Deuteronomy 34:10).* This sentence describes a person with an active, vibrant faith. To know God face to face, ask Him to strengthen your faith as you talk with Him daily, walk with Him through the pages of Holy Scripture, sit with Him at His table on a regular basis, and visit with Him often in His house.

God's Words of Encouragement

Blessed are those who have learned to acclaim You, who walk in the light of Your presence, O LORD. They rejoice in Your name all day long; they exalt in Your righteousness. For You are their glory and strength, and by Your favor you exalt our horn. *Psalm 89:15–17*

Our help is in the name of the LORD, the Maker of heaven and earth. *Psalm 124:8*

In all these things we are more than conquerors through Him who loved us. For I am convinced that neither death nor life, neither angels nor demons, neither the present nor the future, nor any powers, neither height nor depth, nor anything else in all creation, will be able to separate us from the love of God that is in Christ Jesus our Lord. *Romans 8:37–39*

So whether you eat or drink or whatever you do, do it all for the glory of God. *1 Corinthians 10:31*

[God said,] "This is the covenant I will make with the house of Israel after that time, declares the Lord. I will put my laws in their minds and write them on their hearts. I will be their God, and they will be my people. *Hebrews 8:10*

✳

A Million-Dollar Bird

I heard the following story in a sermon. Its illustration of God's great love has always impressed me.

Two dirty, tattered children spent their time hunting for birds to torture. Whenever they found such hapless birds, they put them into an old rusty cage. Then they would poke the birds mercilessly with sharp sticks. While the birds were in the cage, they received no food or water.

One day, a kind old man met the two children. With great sadness he observed how they mistreated the birds trapped in their cage. "Why are you doing this?" he asked.

"We love to torture birds," the children replied.

The kind old man looked at the miserable birds. Then to the surprise of the children, the man said, "I would like to buy the birds." The children laughed at the offer. What would an old man want with such ugly, mistreated birds?

"What will you pay?" the children asked in greedy tones.

With great compassion the kind old man looked at the birds. "I will pay one million dollars for each bird," the man replied.

The children laughed with glee at such misjudgment of value and yelled, "Sold!"

The kind old man took the cage with the birds in it and proceeded to walk up a high hill. The pathway was lined with lush green trees and fragrant flowers. The song of birds filled the azure sky, and the rushing water of nearby streams lent an atmosphere of peace.

At the top of the hill, the kind old man opened the cage and set the birds free. At first the miserable creatures sat on the ground as though they doubted their freedom. The old man waved his hand and encouraged them to fly away and claim their new life. One after another the birds took flight into their delightful surroundings.

What a poignant story, and yet it's only a glimpse of how much God loved you—enough to send His Son, Jesus, as your Savior. What a tremendous price He paid for your sins—His life! And now you enjoy the freedom of new life in Him through your Baptism. Praise God for His great mercy!

God's Words of Encouragement

As a father has compassion on his children, so the LORD has compassion on those who fear Him. *Psalm 103:13*

O Lord, You are my God; I will exalt You and praise Your name, for in perfect faithfulness You have done marvelous things, things planned long ago. … On this mountain He will destroy the shroud that enfolds all peoples, … He will swallow up death forever. The Sovereign LORD will wipe away the tears from all faces; He will remove the disgrace of His people from all the earth. *Isaiah 25:1, 7–8*

"I, the LORD, have called you in righteousness; I will take hold of your hand. I will keep you and will make you to be a covenant for the people and a light for the Gentiles." *Isaiah 42:6*

[The Lord says,] "Fear not, for I have redeemed you; I have summoned you by name; you are mine." *Isaiah 43:1*

[The Lord says,] "Then you will find your joy in the LORD, and I will cause you to ride on the heights of the land and to feast on the inheritance of your father Jacob." *Isaiah 58:14*

I delight greatly in the LORD; my soul rejoices in my God. For He has clothed me with garments of salvation and arrayed me in a robe of righteousness, as a bridegroom adorns his head like a priest, and as a bride adorns herself with her jewels. *Isaiah 61:10*

In Him we have redemption through His blood, the forgiveness of sins, in accordance with the riches of God's grace that He lavished on us with all wisdom and understanding. *Ephesians 1:7–8*

✳

The Aquarium

Good stories intrigue children. Storytelling is an essential element of successful teaching. Many years have passed since I first heard this story.

A man decided to decorate his room with a large, expensive aquarium. A lot of money went into adding colorful, decorative accessories so the fish might enjoy their beautiful home. Once the man was satisfied that the aquarium was ready, he bought expensive exotic fish. Each day he spent hours watching the fish as they enjoyed the grandeur of their new home. He fed his fish the best fish foods, including bits of sweet shrimp. The aquarium became the delight of his life.

One day, to his dismay, the man noticed the water of the aquarium churning violently as two fish engaged in fierce combat. Although there was sufficient food, the two fish were fighting over a particular piece of sweet shrimp. The skirmish ended, and the man hoped such a fight would not happen again. The next day, however, other fish began to behave aggressively toward each other. For no apparent reason, they attacked each other and tore at each other's shiny scales. Soon some of his expensive fish were floating on the top of the water, dead.

The man was horrified as he watched the senseless fighting. He pleaded with them to stop fighting. Pounding on the glass sides of the aquarium did nothing to distract the fish from their ugly behavior. He put his hand in the water to separate the fish that were fighting, but instead of stopping, they tore at his hand until it bled. The man wondered if he should dump out the water and destroy his aquarium.

As the man shed great tears of sorrow, a plan entered his mind. He would have to become one of them. He would become a fish. Perhaps in this way he could live with them and talk some sense into their silly heads.

Placing himself on the edge of the great aquarium, the man slowly changed into a tiny fish egg. He dropped off the edge, into the water, and floated down to the bottom of the aquarium where he hid under a shell. There he stayed until he hatched. Now he was a fish like the others, yet he was not just a fish but also the man who loved them.

As he grew bigger, he ventured into the open waters of the aquarium. The fish paid little attention to him until he tried to stop their fighting. They resented him and thought he had no business telling them how they should behave. The more he warned them, the more the fish attacked him. They tore open his sides and ripped off his beautiful fins until the water became bloody. One day, the man who had become a fish died because the fish could not tolerate his presence in the aquarium.

The man who became a fish did what he could to show the fish that he loved them.

But there's a little problem with this allegory, isn't there? There's no resurrection! We can be thankful that God in His grace completed this story. He raised Jesus from the dead to show Himself as the victor over sin, death, and the devil.

God's Words of Encouragement

Restore to me the joy of Your salvation and grant me a willing spirit, to sustain me. Then I will teach transgressors Your ways, and sinners will turn back to You. *Psalm 51:12–13*

The LORD is compassionate and gracious, slow to anger, abounding in love. … He does not treat us as our sins deserve or repay us according to our iniquities. For as high as the heavens are above the earth, so great is His love for those who fear Him. *Psalm 103:8, 10*

The LORD is good to all; He has compassion on all He has made. … They will tell of the glory of Your kingdom and speak of Your might, so that all men may know of Your mighty acts and the glorious splendor of Your kingdom. *Psalm 145:9, 11–12*

For you know the grace of our Lord Jesus Christ, that though He was rich, yet for your sakes He became poor, so that you through His poverty might become rich. *2 Corinthians 8:9*

Here is a trustworthy saying that deserves full acceptance: Christ Jesus came into the world to save sinners—of whom I am the worst. But for that very reason I was shown mercy so that in me, the worst of sinners, Christ Jesus might display His unlimited patience as an example for those who would believe on Him and receive eternal life. *1 Timothy 1:15–16*

Praise be to the God and Father of our Lord Jesus Christ! In His great mercy He has given us new birth into a living hope through the resurrection of Jesus Christ from the dead, and into an inheritance that can never perish, spoil or fade—kept in heaven for you, who through faith are shielded by God's power. *1 Peter 1:3–5*

If we claim to be without sin, we deceive ourselves and the truth is not in us. If we confess our sins, He is faithful and just and will forgive us our sins and purify us from all unrighteousness. *1 John 1:8–10*

I am coming soon. Hold on to what you have, so that no one will take your crown. Him who overcomes I will make a pillar in the temple of my God. Never again will he leave it. I will write on him the name of my God and the name of the city of my God, the new Jerusalem, which is coming down out of heaven from my God; and I will also write on him My new name. *Revelation 3:11–12*

*

Teacher Baggage

Everyone brings something of their past into adult life. The past contributes many positive experiences, but the past also may include baggage, even dysfunction, that can affect the Christian professional.

Parents often comment that their children imitate them. Children may be referred to as "chips off the old block." It's only natural that experiences during your childhood, your most impressionable years, would become a part of you.

What baggage do you carry with you from your childhood? Perhaps you weren't allowed to be inquisitive or adventurous. Maybe you never suffered the natural consequences of your actions or maybe you were punished for every minor rule infraction. You may have been allowed to run wild or you may have been prevented from exploring your boundaries. Whatever your childhood excesses or limitations, they affect how you react to your students today.

The light of parental expectations shines brightly on you, revealing your many gifts and exposing your inevitable flaws. How do you handle your baggage? First, admit that such baggage exists. Identify it. Apologize to God and to those you may have wronged because of actions or attitudes you carry with you from your childhood. God will forgive you for Jesus' sake, and He will help you find solutions. He will lead you to the best sources of help and affirmation. He helps you sift through your training, advice from colleagues, past experiences, student reactions, and parental comments to find those ideas and activities that truly help you shed your baggage.

God's Words of Encouragement

May Your unfailing love rest upon us, O LORD, even as we put our hope in You. *Psalm 33:22*

God is our refuge and strength, an ever-present help in trouble. *Psalm 46:1*

I pray that out of [the Father's] glorious riches He may strengthen you with power through His Spirit in your inner being, so that Christ may dwell in your hearts through faith. And I pray that you, being rooted and established in love, may have power, together with all the saints, to grasp how wide and long and high and deep is the love of Christ. *Ephesians 3:16–18*

Do everything without complaining or arguing, so that you may become blameless and pure, children of God without fault in a crooked and depraved generation, in which you shine like stars in the universe as you hold out the word of life. *Philippians 2:14–16*

And whatever you do, whether in word or deed, do it all in the name of the Lord Jesus, giving thanks to God the Father through Him. *Colossians 3:17*

The Lord's servant must not quarrel; instead, he must be kind to everyone, able to teach, not resentful. *2 Timothy 2:24*

Everyone should be quick to listen, slow to speak and slow to become angry, ... and humbly accept the word planted in you, which can save you. *James 1:19, 21*

*

Stuck in a Broken World

It doesn't take long to find out that you teach in a broken world. Although you may be in a Christian setting, you still experience varying degrees of brokenness. The world's brokenness displays itself in meaninglessness, cynicism, despair, ill will, gossip, guilt, double standards, belittling, dysfunction, and in many other ways. But perhaps the greatest example of this brokenness is people's efforts to serve themselves.

But you have the answer to the world's broken nature. The Christian teacher has the answer for parents' cries for help. The Christian teacher opens the door to God's love, to God's plan of salvation for the world—Jesus Christ. As you share His Word in your classroom, God moves into your students' lives. Over the world's sin-filled rubble, God builds a home in the hearts of His people. Through your words, God's compassion revealed through Jesus Christ may reach for the first time into the lives of people. The Holy Spirit will work the fertile ground and plant the seed of faith.

As you begin this day or this week or this school year, pray the prayer of Solomon:

O Lord God, You have made me a teacher to these children. Give me wisdom and knowledge. Grant me an understanding of their needs and compassion for their souls.

Your ministry to a broken world is not a road paved with honor and praise. Some students and parents may rejoice in their presence in a Christian school. Others may not joyfully embrace a Christian education. Old habits and former lifestyles can challenge your expectations of responsibility and a spiritual commitment. Spiritual commitment may not even exist if parents seek out a Christian school as a haven from social problems rather than as an opportunity to strengthen their child's relationship with God.

When a Christian school realizes its purpose and potential, it generates joy and vitality. You and your colleagues know your ministry has an eternal benefit. You can focus on the good instead of the bad. You can daily deal with your students under the direction of Jesus Christ. Through you, Jesus reaches out to His lambs and gathers them in His arms.

God's Words of Encouragement

From heaven the LORD looks down and sees all mankind; from His dwelling place He watches all who live on earth. *Psalm 33:13–14*

But those who hope in the LORD will renew their strength. They will soar on wings like eagles; they will run and not grow weary, they will walk and not be faint. *Isaiah 40:31*

The Spirit of the Sovereign LORD is on me, because the LORD has anointed me to preach good news to the poor. He has sent me to bind up the brokenhearted, to proclaim freedom for the captives and release from darkness for the prisoners, to proclaim the year of the LORD's favor and the day of vengeance of our God. *Isaiah 61:1–2*

As God's fellow workers we urge you not to receive God's

grace in vain. For He says, "In the time of My favor I heard you, and in the day of salvation I helped you." I tell you, now is the time of God's favor, now is the day of salvation. *2 Corinthians 6:1–2*

Therefore put on the full armor of God, so that when the day of evil comes, you may be able to stand your ground, and after you have done everything, to stand. ... And pray in the Spirit on all occasions with all kinds of prayers and requests. With this in mind, be alert and always keep on praying for all the saints. *Ephesians 6:13, 18*

Let the word of Christ dwell in you richly as you teach and admonish one another with all wisdom. *Colossians 3:16*

*

First Love

In Revelation 2:4, John is instructed to write to the angel of the church in Ephesus, "Yet I hold this against you: You have forsaken your first love." Can you identify with this statement?

Just think about how easily something becomes commonplace when you're around it all the time. When you get a new car, you park it far away from other cars and tell people to be careful not to scratch it. When you paint a room, you tell your children to keep their hands off the walls. But what happens? Your car probably would smile just to get washed, and the living-room walls need another paint job to cover the smudges. You've lost some of that initial concern—that first love.

Losing that first love also can be a problem for teachers. Worship services in the same church every Sunday and chapel day may become less meaningful, and the sounds of praise may become ordinary. Colleagues that you teach with year after year may become old hat. Even over the course of the year, students can become part of the routine, and you may pass over their presence without notice until they mess up. You don't approach the school or your classroom with that same eager step as you did that first day.

Sin tempts you to become less concerned, to become tired and weary. Satan wears you down through routine and repetition. You begin to worship the business of teaching, and God loses out. Keeping that first love alive is a job for the Holy Spirit. He works to renew your faith and your dedication to God. The Spirit reminds you of your calling, of your love of teaching others. Through the Spirit's work, your joy and love of the ministry is restored.

Ask God to keep you from losing your first love for Him or your love for your calling, your colleagues, or your students.

God's Words of Encouragement

[God said,] "I remember the devotion of your youth, how as a bride you loved Me and followed Me through the desert, through a land not sown. What fault did your fathers find in Me, that they strayed so far from Me?" *Jeremiah 2:2, 5*

" 'For I know the plans I have for you,' declares the LORD, 'plans to prosper you and not to harm you, plans to give you hope and a future. Then you will call upon Me and come and pray to Me, and I will listen to you. You will seek Me and find Me when you seek Me with all your heart.' " *Jeremiah 29:11–13*

[Jesus said,] "Because of the increase of wickedness, the love of most will grow cold, but he who stands firm to the end will be saved." *Matthew 24:12–13*

Therefore, since through God's mercy we have this ministry, we do not lose heart. *2 Corinthians 4:1*

God, who said, "Let light shine out of darkness," made His light shine in our hearts to give us the light of the knowledge of the glory of God in the face of Christ. But we have this treasure in jars of clay to show that this all-surpassing power is from God and not from us. *2 Corinthians 4:6–7*

For this reason I remind you to fan into flame the gift of God, which is in you through the laying on of my hands. For God did not give us a spirit of timidity, but a spirit of power, of love and of self-discipline. *2 Timothy 1:6–7*

Come near to God and He will come near to you. *James 4:8*

Yet I hold this against you: You have forsaken your first love. Remember the height from which you have fallen! Repent and do the things you did at first. *Revelation 2:4–5*

I know your deeds; you have a reputation of being alive, but you are dead. Wake up! Strengthen what remains and is about to die, for I have not found your deeds complete in the sight of my God. Remember, therefore, what you have received and heard; obey it, and repent. *Revelation 3:1–3*

*

Teacher Shock

Did you realize how much would be expected of you as a teacher? Perhaps you were shocked that first month or year as more and more expectations crawled out of the woodwork. Job descriptions lengthen as congregational agendas, school board handbooks, staff handbooks, parent handbooks, orientation meetings, staff meetings, disasters, whims, and unwritten agendas make their demands on you. You discovered that the more skills you had, the more you were asked to do.

It can be disastrous to allow a teacher to remain in shock, especially a shock caused by work overload. Those in charge need to be on the lookout for signs of stress and burnout. Discuss your feelings with a valued colleague who will listen to and support you. Explain to your principal or school board that you can roll with the punches if consideration is given to limiting the number of extra responsibilities, and to matching extra duties with your abilities and interests.

Modern schools extend beyond the classroom to clubs, sports teams, latch-key programs, special events, tutoring, counseling, meetings, and accreditation preparation. Most of these responsibilities are inescapable but your staff should work together to schedule these extras and minimize teacher shock.

But what happens when you do become overloaded? Speak truthfully in love and state your feelings honestly. God has given you a gift—the gift of teaching. If you demonstrate a caring nature, if your classroom is your top priority, if you strive for excellence in your profession, and if you are a team player, your gift is being used wisely. God did not call you to do everything in the church. He is as concerned about your mental and physical health as He is about your spiritual health. Pick which extra activities you want to be involved with and politely but firmly say no to the rest. Explain that God's gift to you is to teach, not to play the organ or serve as the church's treasurer.

As you experience times of overload, lean back into God's hands. He has promised to carry your anxieties and help with your problems. He invites you to call upon Him in every trouble. God will guide you through the hectic times and lead you to green pastures and quiet waters.

God's Words of Encouragement

He makes me lie down in green pastures, He leads me beside quiet waters, He restores my soul. *Psalm 23:2–3*

[Jesus] said to [the apostles], "Come with Me by yourselves to a quiet place and get some rest." *Mark 6:31*

It was He who gave some to be apostles, some to be prophets, some to be evangelists, and some to be pastors and teachers, to prepare God's people for works of service, so that the body of Christ may be built up. *Ephesians 4:11*

We continually remember before our God and Father your work produced by faith, your labor prompted by love, and your endurance inspired by hope in our Lord Jesus Christ. *1 Thessalonians 1:3*

Be joyful always; pray continually; give thanks in all circumstances, for this is God's will for you in Christ Jesus.

49

Do not put out the Spirit's fire. *1 Thessalonians 5:16–19*

Prepare your minds for action; be self-controlled; set your hope fully on the grace to be given you when Jesus Christ is revealed. *1 Peter 1:13*

Cast all your anxiety on [Jesus] because He cares for you. *1 Peter 5:7*

What Have I Done with God's Gifts?

Toddlers have a short attention span. You give them something and as soon as they see something else, they want it. After all the Christmas gifts are open, a toddler's attention shifts from one toy to the next without spending much time playing with any one of the gifts. The child inevitably wants what someone else has. "You play with what you have" is the usual exasperated reply.

Are you a spiritual toddler? Do you ask God for more without responsibly using what God has already given you? Consider the gift of faith. How do you treat this gift? Does your life reflect God's presence in your heart? Do you have a regular and fervent prayer life? Do you have a spiritual life? Are you quick to praise and thank God, even in the midst of troubles? Do you read and study His Word daily? Do you pray as Jesus' disciples did, "Lord, increase my faith"?

What have you done with God's gift of health? Do you take care of yourself? Do you seek to glorify God by staying physically fit in appreciation and celebration of the body He has given you? Does your good health demonstrate itself in a productive life?

God made a world with great variety, but to His human creatures He gave the gift of emotion. What have you done with this gift? Have your emotions matured as your body has? Do they function on an adult level? Do you allow your emotions to control your life? God gave us

51

love, the greatest emotion, and His Word emphasizes love's importance as a vital ingredient in life. Do you cultivate a loving life? Do you allow love to make you sensitive to the needs of others? Does your capacity to love move you to action? Is your love guided by God's words, "Do to others as you would have them do to you"?

During your lifetime, God will make you the steward of wealth and riches. How do you react to this responsibility? Do you feel you have earned this wealth on your own? Do you give God His portion joyfully, as a thank offering for His many gifts? Do you horde your riches because you doubt God's providence?

God's world expresses His creativity. As the crown of His creation, He has given you creativity. Do you accept creativity as a gift from God? Do you seek creative solutions or look for appropriate outlets for your creativity? For teachers, every lesson plan is an opportunity for creativity. Are your plans creative or are they part of a repetitious system, one that requires little thought or imagination on your part?

Some of God's gifts apply directly to Christians, particularly the gift of concern for souls. Christians care whether others believe in Jesus as their Savior. When you look at your students, do you see only children or do you also see souls that need to hear the Gospel message? Do you share your faith with those who do not know about Jesus? Do you help young believers learn more about God and His salvation plan? Do you include parents in your realm of spiritual care and concern? Do you help your school reach out to its community with the Good News of Jesus? Do you discuss with your class the spiritual needs of your country and the world? Do you find ways to reach faraway places with the Gospel?

God has given you so much. What have you done with what God has given you? On your own, you can do nothing to please God or use what He has given you wisely. Ask God to send His Holy Spirit to strengthen you and equip you to wisely use all of His good gifts to you.

God's Words of Encouragement

Then I acknowledged my sin to You and did not cover up my iniquity. I said, "I will confess my transgressions to the LORD"—and You forgave the guilt of my sin. *Psalm 32:5*

A happy heart makes the face cheerful, but heartache crushes the spirit. *Proverbs 15:13*

Be very careful, then, how you live—not as unwise but as wise, making the most of every opportunity. *Ephesians 5:15–16*

Only let us live up to what we have already attained. *Philippians 3:16*

But you, man of God, flee from all this, and pursue righteousness, godliness, faith, love, endurance and gentleness. *1 Timothy 6:11*

Every good and perfect gift is from above, coming down from the Father of the heavenly lights, who does not change like shifting shadows. *James 1:17*

Have You Taken All Your Vitamins This Morning?

For those who take vitamins, their morning ritual includes carefully swallowing every tablet thought to be necessary, often in a precise order. When facing the new school day, a Christian teacher can also carefully follow certain routines. The Lord has made this day, and He invites us to rejoice and be glad in it.

The new day demands attention, enthusiasm, a new supply of courage, and a renewed sense of purpose. Preparing for these demands takes time, so rule number 1 is to spend time with God. Teachers who faithfully take their spiritual vitamins find time to sit and talk to God. You can offer your prayer list before God's throne. Or you can read a devotion and meditate on God's Word. As you prepare for school, talk with God as you shower, make breakfast, travel to school, and open up your classroom. God will answer your request to bless your day.

Rule number 2 is don't skip breakfast. An empty stomach can't provide you with the necessary energy to be a good teacher. Don't let a growling stomach destroy a good mood. The vitamin of respect for your body's needs will contribute to your sense of well-being.

Rule number 3 is straightforward—always be prepared. Students can sense your uneasiness if you walk in late, hurry through lessons, question where materials are, or apologize often for a lack of preparation. To avoid being a "barely-made-it" teacher requires advance preparation.

The preparation vitamin ensures your enjoyment of teaching and your eagerness to be in the classroom. Ask God to bless your plans. Then trust that He will be there to help you carry out your plans successfully. As you plan, don't forget to consider options to employ if you don't seem to be communicating well with students or parents.

As you walk into your classroom, know that God goes with you. Talk to Him. Ask Him to bless your work with His lambs. Request an extra measure of wisdom to discern your students' special needs. Always thank God for the opportunity to be a Christian teacher.

Make sure that meaningful morning devotions set the mood in your classroom. The devotion will encourage you and your students as you live for and with God. Read God's Word. Share your faith. Praise God. Include confession and forgiveness. Pray for and with each other. The morning devotion will help students realize what it means to be a part of God's family—a child of God.

God's Words of Encouragement

In the morning, O LORD, You hear my voice; in the morning I lay my requests before You and wait in expectation. *Psalm 5:3*

He will command His angels concerning you to guard you in all your ways; they will lift you up in their hands, so that you will not strike your foot against a stone. *Psalm 91:11–12*

This is the day the LORD has made; let us rejoice and be glad in it. *Psalm 118:24*

Do your best to present yourself to God as one approved, a workman who does not need to be ashamed and who correctly handles the word of truth. *2 Timothy 2:15*

Be patient and stand firm, because the Lord's coming is near. *James 5:8*

✳

The Process of Life

The term *process* implies a continual development over a period of time. It also indicates that changes are made to the product. Life is a process, both consciously and unconsciously. You make a conscious effort to develop a certain skill or to work through a given situation. You also experience life as a process when you unconsciously respond in times of crisis and discover later the changes that event produced in your life.

The process of life always happens under God's direction. You can consciously ask God to help you make a decision, to find a solution, or to help you develop skills for a specific task. In those circumstances where you ask for God's guidance, you may not always be aware of God's gradual shaping of your life. But you have invited Him to be part of the process of life, and you can be assured He is.

God does not desert His children. He uses life's events to teach and reteach you. He uses your thought processes, His Word, and other people to guide your actions and words. Through faith, God has instilled in you a dedication that sets you apart as His special servant—a teacher. God promises answers and blessings to those who seek His will for their lives. He will shape and affirm you as His servant.

The process of life will include painful experiences. Vindictive people can make your life miserable. They start negative criticism and share it with anybody who will listen. You will remember these painful experiences for a lifetime. It's difficult to be patient under adversity, but you won't face times like these alone. Confess any mistakes you made to your Lord and to those you wronged. Speak the truth firmly, love the vindictive individuals, and leave the results in God's hands. He will act in your best interest and strengthen you for the path He lays before you. God will not leave your side. In the Christian pilgrimage there are no crowns without crosses.

As part of the conscious aspect of life's process, give honest answers to these questions. Do I enjoy teaching or is it just a job? Do I like dealing with students? Am I builder or a demolisher? Do students appreciate me as a teacher? Do I share my faith? Do I appreciate my colleagues? Do I manage my time well? Do I prepare adequately? Are my students receiving an excellent education? Am I involved in the ministry of the school *and* church? Am I a team player? Do I keep communication lines open with other people? Do I look for the good in people and then encourage them? Am I willing to go the extra mile? Is Jesus my mentor? Can I list examples that show my professional improvement? Can I identify areas that still need improvement? Am I willing to extend my professional training? Do I respect myself? Do I take care of my health and my personal spiritual life?

From these questions, you can see the importance of your own life process and how it impacts others. Because God is the catalyst for your life process, He will bless you and make you a blessing to others.

God's Words of Encouragement
You anoint my head with oil; my cup overflows. Surely

goodness and love will follow me all the days of my life, and I will dwell in the house of the LORD forever. *Psalm 23:5–6*

O Lord, hear my voice. Let Your ears be attentive to my cry for mercy. *Psalm 130:2*

Oh, the depth of the riches of the wisdom and knowledge of God! How unsearchable His judgments, and His paths beyond tracing out! … For from Him and through Him and to Him are all things. To Him be the glory forever! Amen. *Romans 11:33, 36*

I know whom I have believed, and am convinced that He is able to guard what I have entrusted to Him for that day. *2 Timothy 1:12*

Dear friends, since God so loves us, we also ought to love one another. *1 John 4:11*

"I am the Alpha and the Omega, the Beginning and the End. To him who is thirsty I will give to drink without cost from the spring of the water of life. He who overcomes will inherit all this, and I will be his God and he will be My son." *Revelation 21:6–7*

✳

When Emotions Take Over

Emotions take over when they are allowed to rule our lives. Emotions aren't bad, in fact they are helpful indicators in life. They add pizazz to our daily existence. They should not control life, however. This is easier said than done, though, because emotions, particularly strong ones, have a habit of haunting us.

Emotions begin to plague your mind as you lose control. For example, a disruptive and willful student causes daily problems that you find difficult to discipline or diffuse. Then the student's parent stops in repeatedly to complain about your teaching methods and especially about your efforts to discipline the child. Your emotions may take over as you are made to feel less and less capable. You might become less tolerant in the classroom and withdrawn when approached by parents or colleagues.

As emotions increase their control, doubts and blame infiltrate the mind. You may blame yourself or others for your emotional reactions, whether positive or negative. Insecurity, frustration, anger, and dislike may begin to affect your work. Runaway emotions can cancel out common sense and patience as you deal with symptoms rather than causes.

Getting to the cause of your emotional upheaval involves an honest evaluation and a prayerful consideration of the facts. Go back to the source, the giver of your emotions, God. He knows that human emotions are not as He intended them. They too have been affected by sin.

In fact, Satan enjoys using emotions to counter God's plans for His people. Ask God to help you take responsibility for your emotions and to find a solution. Consider the following prayer as a starting point for your discussion with God about your emotions:

> Lord, You know that I have strong emotions. Right now they are destroying my joy and satisfaction as a teacher. I do not have the strength to understand or to make the necessary changes in my emotional life. I ask You, out of Your great mercy, to lead me to the solution. I give this problem to You. I ask You to forgive me for Jesus' sake for the times I lost control. Assure me of Your continued presence in my life. Give me a calm spirit that trusts in Your daily help. May the expression of my emotions bring glory to You. In my Savior's name. Amen.

Do not overlook your colleagues. They can minister to you, but only if you share your problem with them. God has given them experiences that may offer simple but amazing ways to handle your emotions. God has given them faith, and they can share their trust in Him. Colleagues who care will also lift your needs to God's throne. When God is sought, trusted, and glorified, you can be sure that He will help.

God's Words of Encouragement

Send forth Your light and Your truth, let them guide me; let them bring me to Your holy mountain, to the place where You dwell. *Psalm 43:3*

"Be still, and know that I am God; I will be exalted among

61

the nations, I will be exalted in the earth." The LORD Almighty is with us; the God of Jacob is our fortress. *Psalm 46:10–11*

[Jesus said,] "I am the vine; you are the branches. If a man remains in Me and I in him, he will bear much fruit; apart from Me you can do nothing." *John 15:5*

The Spirit helps us in our weakness. We do not know what we ought to pray for, but the Spirit Himself intercedes for us with groans that words cannot express. *Romans 8:26*

May the God of hope fill you with all joy and peace as you trust in Him, so that you may overflow with hope by the power of the Holy Spirit. *Romans 15:13*

Humble yourselves before the Lord, and He will lift you up. *James 4:10*

＊

The Big Picture

When life fills our agendas with a variety of responsibilities, we tend to focus only on what is personally important and fulfilling. It's easy for teachers to do this. Your classroom is your primary responsibility and it deserves careful attention. It can keep you from being concerned about anything else.

When your focus is too narrow, you miss the big picture. What about the needs of your colleagues? What about the needs of other students in the school? While you set your goals and objectives for your classroom, be aware that the staff, the school board, and the congregation have goals also.

Recognize that God has placed you on a team that is competing on a much larger playing field than just your classroom. Operating in isolation will not meet God's desires for His team—communicating the salvation message to all people.

Catch the joy and challenge of working as part of the big picture. It can be satisfying and exciting to work toward mutual goals and to be involved with a team with a vision. And the big picture will only enhance your personal involvement in your classroom.

God's Words of Encouragement

Unless the LORD builds the house, its builders labor in vain. Unless the LORD watches over the city, the watchmen stand guard in vain. *Psalm 127:1*

Therefore, I urge you, brothers, in view of God's mercy, to offer your bodies as living sacrifices, holy and pleasing to God—this is your spiritual act of worship. *Romans 12:1*

For none of us lives to himself alone and none of us dies to himself alone. If we live, we live to the Lord; and if we die, we die to the Lord. So, whether we live or die, we belong to the Lord. *Romans 14:7–8*

"As surely as I live," says the Lord, "every knee will bow before Me; every tongue will confess to God." So then, each of us will give an account of himself to God. *Romans 14:11–12*

I planted the seed, Apollos watered it, but God made it grow. So neither he who plants nor he who waters is anything, but only God, who makes things grow. *1 Corinthians 3:6*

We are therefore Christ's ambassadors, as though God were making His appeal through us. *2 Corinthians 5:20*

Forgetting what is behind and straining toward what is ahead, I press on toward the goal to win the prize for which God has called me heavenward in Christ Jesus. *Philippians 3:13–14*

He who has an ear, let him hear what the Spirit says to the churches. To him who overcomes, I will give some of the hidden manna. I will also give him a white stone with a new name written on it, known only to him who receives it. *Revelation 2:17*

*

If You're a Crow, Don't Act Like a Pigeon

If you are a young, inexperienced teacher, you might attempt to pattern yourself after a colleague you admire. I fell into that trap myself. I reasoned that if I could be like this teacher I admired, my success would be secure. It didn't work. I was a crow, and he was a pigeon.

God creates individuals. Just look at some flowers. The flower's seeds contain the instructions for the shape, color, scent, and the season for blooming. If a sunflower is planted in a rose garden, it won't grow or look like a rose.

In 1 Corinthians 12:18–20, the apostle Paul writes:

But in fact God has arranged the parts in the body, every one of them, just as He wanted them to be. If they were all one part, where would the body be? As it is, there are many parts, but one body.

God's creativity gave each of us different gifts, even teachers. Some teachers present great lessons. Some have fantastic rapport with their students. Some can make everyone laugh. Some teachers have an empathetic spirit and can provide care in times of crisis.

Do you know who you are? Ask God to guide you to His purpose for your work. He will reveal to you the special abilities and characteristics He has given to you to carry out the jobs He has planned for you. If you are a crow, act like a crow. If you are a pigeon, act like a pigeon.

65

God's Words of Encouragement

Commit your way to the LORD; trust in Him and He will do this: He will make your righteousness shine like the dawn, the justice of your cause like the noonday sun. *Psalm 37:5–6*

And we know that in all things God works for the good of those who love Him. *Romans 8:28*

"My grace is sufficient for you, for My power is made perfect in weakness." Therefore I will boast all the more gladly about my weaknesses, so that Christ's power may rest on me. *2 Corinthians 12:9*

But the fruit of the Spirit is love, joy, peace, patience, kindness, goodness, faithfulness, gentleness and self-control. Against such things there is no law. Those who belong to Christ Jesus have crucified the sinful nature with its passions and desires. Since we live by the Spirit, let us keep in step with the Spirit. *Galatians 5:22–25*

Conduct yourselves in a manner worthy of the gospel of Christ. Then ... I will know that you stand firm in one spirit, contending as one man for the faith of the gospel. *Philippians 1:27*

All of us who are mature should take such a view of things. And if on some point you think differently, that too God will make clear to you. *Philippians 3:15*

Be strong in the grace that is in Christ Jesus. And the things you have heard me say in the presence of many witnesses entrust to reliable men who will also be qualified to teach others. *2 Timothy 2:1–2*

Faith by itself, if it is not accompanied by action, is dead. *James 2:17*

*

God, Please Fix It

During my association with Christian schools, I worked with several gifted handymen. At first, I made the major mistake of telling these men how to make items or how to fix others. I came to realize that their ideas were far better than mine. After that, we briefly discussed a task, they indicated how it might be done, and then they did it.

It's foolhardy to approach God like I approached the handymen and say, "God, here are my plans, now please bless them and make them happen." Remember that God is all-wise, sovereign, and He loves you unconditionally. His plans are always so much better than yours. You can safely say, "Lord, direct me according to Your will." God knows how to fix things.

Even though God doesn't need specifics, some areas of our prayer life need to be clearly defined. We should confess particular sins so that God can assure us of His forgiveness for Jesus' sake. We can take specific problems to God and communicate the yearnings in our hearts. Then we can release these issues to God's control. One of the uses of prayer is to communicate our desire for the Lord's counsel on a particular issue. Through prayer, we can specifically request God to tune us in to His plan for our lives. What a comfort to know that even when we don't see where God is moving us, He knows what's best and, in His wisdom and love, accomplishes His plan. We can confidently pray, "God, please fix it."

God's Words of Encouragement

Teach me Your way, O LORD; lead me in a straight path. *Psalm 27:11*

Delight yourself in the LORD and He will give you the desires of your heart. *Psalm 37:4*

Blessed is the man who makes the LORD his trust. *Psalm 40:4*

But I am like an olive tree flourishing in the house of God; I trust in God's unfailing love for ever and ever. *Psalm 52:8*

Trust in the LORD with all your heart and lean not on your own understanding. *Proverbs 3:5*

Many are the plans in a man's heart, but it is the LORD's purpose that prevails. *Proverbs 19:21*

The LORD is good, a refuge in times of trouble. He cares for those who trust in Him. *Nahum 1:7*

[Jesus said,] "This, then, is how you should pray: 'Our Father in heaven, … Your will be done on earth as it is in heaven.' " *Matthew 6:9–10*

Going a little farther, [Jesus] fell with His face to the ground and prayed, "My Father, if it is possible, may this cup be taken from Me. Yet not as I will, but as You will." *Matthew 26:39*

But the Lord is faithful, and He will strengthen and protect you from the evil one. *2 Thessalonians 3:3*

*

Just a Teacher

I wanted to be a musician who could make a pipe organ breathe fire. I wanted to conduct choirs that would make the angels jealous. But much to the disappointment of my college counselor (who thought every teacher should be a musician), I just didn't have any musical talent. After attending piano or organ recitals at the college, I immediately went to practice, hoping that what I had heard would somehow come out of klutzy fingers. But I still didn't have "it." I also discovered I wasn't comfortable teaching sports or refereeing games. And when it came to art, my abilities were far from those of a skilled artisan.

So I ended up being "just a teacher." But what's wrong with that? I enjoyed planning lessons, and I loved to teach. What joy it brought me to help a student who was stuck. What a challenge it was to explain concepts so that students really understood. Working with a class really excited me. It was fun to see students learn new skills, think through processes, grasp new concepts. Nothing was more fulfilling than to watch a student approach my desk with a gleam in the eye and say, "Wanna see what I did?" I learned to enjoy being "just a teacher."

If I had been a hotshot musician, would I have done as much counseling with parents and students? I might have lost all those opportunities to listen, develop programs, or set up systems to help students and families work through their problems. I wouldn't have spent as much time on lesson preparation or refining my teaching technique.

Some of us are called to be "just a teacher." While it took time for me to realize this, I eventually came to enjoy letting others play the organ, or conduct the choir, or coach the teams, or produce the artwork. God brought me to the point where I derived tremendous satisfaction from being me—a unique individual with unique talents given to me by my heavenly Father. God brought many students into my classroom, and I know they have learned about the world and, more importantly, about their Savior and God. It's amazing how God put me in the right position to accomplish His goals.

God's Words of Encouragement

Be still before the LORD and wait patiently for Him; do not fret when men succeed in their ways. *Psalm 37:7*

Come and listen, all you who fear God; let me tell you what He has done for me. *Psalm 66:16*

Yet, O LORD, You are our Father. We are the clay, You are the potter; we are all the work of Your hand. *Isaiah 64:8*

What, after all, is Apollos? And what is Paul? Only servants, through whom you came to believe—as the Lord has assigned to each his task. *1 Corinthians 3:5*

Do not neglect your gift. *1 Timothy 4:14*

＊

Would You Like to Resign?

Is classroom discipline too demanding? Are you overloaded, and no one seems to care? Are parents complaining about you? Do you want to improve, but you aren't sure how to go about it? Do you spend so much time fighting the little fires that you can't put out the big blaze? Are you underpaid or struggling financially? Have you honestly evaluated things only to find that your best skills aren't suited to teaching? It's amazing all the stuff college never taught you about teaching. After you've invested time and money to prepare for the profession, is teaching a mistake?

Such thoughts and questions are painful and do little for your self-worth. Whatever you do, don't resign! Ask God to help you evaluate your emotions and questions about the profession. You might consider using the following process. Make three columns on a sheet of paper. In the first column, list symptoms of your problems with teaching. This includes evidence that things aren't going well. In the second column, list the reasons you feel are behind the evidence. In the third column, list possible solutions. Spend time on this. Ask God to bless this process and help you honestly evaluate your situation. He will guide you to the proper answers.

When you're in a crisis, it's doubly important that you surround yourself with people who care about you. Talk to people who you think will give you honest, caring answers. You might discover that your feelings aren't unique. Ask for suggestions. Take feedback as constructive criticism meant to help you improve. Sometimes the point at which you want to resign becomes the point at which you begin to grow. To grow, ask God to make you willing to make changes where possible. Get to the root causes and ask a trusted colleague for help.

Emotions often run high when you hurt. You may even question your faith. Don't let your emotions overwhelm your faith. Pray fervently every day. God will hear your soul's complaint and come to your aid. Trust Him. Seek His counsel. He will not leave you without answers. Learning to pray can be the biggest lesson you learn in times of distress.

Whatever your calling, remember that your choice of vocation is not as important as your ministry to others and whether you glorify God in what you do. As a Christian, you are called to serve the Lord. He will bless your service no matter what you do.

God's Words of Encouragement

Turn to me and be gracious to me, for I am lonely and afflicted. The troubles of my heart have multiplied; free me from my anguish. Look upon my affliction and my distress and take away all my sins. *Psalm 25:16–18*

The LORD is close to the brokenhearted and saves those who are crushed in spirit. *Psalm 34:18*

A cheerful heart is good medicine, but a crushed spirit dries up the bones. *Proverbs 17:22*

All a man's ways seem right to him, but the LORD weighs the heart. *Proverbs 21:2*

And we know that in all things God works for the good of those who love Him, who have been called according to His purpose. *Romans 8:28*

We are hard pressed on every side, but not crushed; perplexed, but not in despair; persecuted, but not abandoned; struck down, but not destroyed. We always carry around in our body the death of Jesus, so that the life of Jesus may also be revealed in our body. *2 Corinthians 4:8–10*

And the God of all grace, who called you to His eternal glory in Christ, after you have suffered a little while, will Himself restore you and make you strong, firm and steadfast. *1 Peter 5:10*

*

Pray for an Open Door

When I graduated from college, I prayed for an open door to a foreign mission field. After teaching in the United States for seven years, I gave up the idea. I felt God had other plans for me. Surprise! Just when my wife and I had concluded that we weren't going, the door opened. Of course, the timing wasn't great for us—we'd just purchased a freezer and a washer and dryer. God often opens doors unexpectedly or when the decision is more difficult.

I still had lessons to learn about open doors even after we moved to Africa. The college where I taught education classes was forced to close its doors because of civil war. The missionaries were sent home. Before the war began, I had written scripts for a radio Gospel broadcast. When the country fell to a communist regime, the station was shut down. The lesson? When God opens a door, take advantage of every precious second. Satan is working just as hard to close the door again.

Upon my return to the United States, I realized the needs of urban schools. I told the Lord that if He would open the door, I was willing to go through it. The Lord opened the door so quickly, I was shocked. This open door called for intense involvement in ministry. It was anything but glamorous, and at times I felt overwhelmed and unsure of my ability to do the tasks God had placed before me. But if God opens the door, He also will provide the strength and blessings to serve.

However, not every open door was for me. I had to

look at myself and the responsibilities of the open door. As I sought God's guidance, He led me to those doors meant for me and pointed me to those positions He had given me the ability to hold.

An open door may not always be in a new location. As a staff, you might pray for an open door in your school. Such a door may be a new program or the addition of a new staff member. Prayers for an open door may reveal a community ministry to the homeless or opportunities to teach the Christian faith or spread the Word of God in countries formerly closed to missionary activity. In Acts, the Christians in Antioch prayed for an open door to the Gentile world. Paul and Barnabas walked through the door God opened and preached the Gospel throughout the Roman empire.

Open doors are exciting. They bring vitality to the Christian witness. They further the kingdom and serve God's people. Pray for them.

God's Words of Encouragement

Let love and faithfulness never leave you; bind them around your neck, write them on the tablet of your heart. *Proverbs 3:3*

[Jesus] told them, "The harvest is plentiful, but the workers are few. Ask the Lord of the harvest, therefore, to send out workers into His harvest field." *Luke 10:2*

[Jesus said,] "Be dressed ready for service and keep your lamps burning, like men waiting for their master to return from a wedding banquet, so that when he comes and knocks they can immediately open the door for him. It will be good for those servants whose master finds them watching when he comes." *Luke 12:35–37*

"My food," said Jesus, "is to do the will of Him who sent me and to finish His work. Do you not say, 'Four months more and then the harvest'? I tell you, open your eyes and look at the fields! They are ripe for harvest." *John 4:34–35*

But I will stay on at Ephesus until Pentecost, because a great door for effective work has opened to me. *1 Corinthians 16:8*

Whatever you do, work at it with all your heart, as working for the Lord, not for men. *Colossians 3:23*

I know your deeds. See, I have placed before you an open door that no one can shut. I know that you have little strength, yet you have kept My word and have not denied My name. *Revelation 3:8*

Here I am! I stand at the door and knock. If anyone hears My voice and opens the door, I will come in and eat with him, and he with Me. *Revelation 3:20*

Exercising in the Wait Room

There are times when you might find yourself unhappy in your present teaching position. "I hope I'm out of here by next year" is your refrain at the end of each day. But here you are, year after year. It seems God is slow in hearing the request of a disgruntled teacher. It's hard to keep exercising in God's wait room when you're tired of exercising. Why doesn't God rescue you?

God doesn't allow problems in your life just to make you miserable. He's working to make you a better vessel. He's firing the clay of your life so that you become strong. Running away from a problem never solves it. In some form, the problem will follow you. When you become disgruntled, consider the story of Pentecost. What a successful day for the Lord and for the apostles. But Peter and the others had spent three rigorous years of training as Jesus' disciples. They had to sit patiently as He explained over and over again His purposes and His message of salvation. When God was ready, they carried out the tasks they had been prepared to do. Our impulsiveness and shortsightedness leads us to believe that we have all the answers. Ask God to give you the skills and servant attitude to accomplish God's plan wherever He places you.

How does the Lord answer disgruntled teachers? The answer might be to stay in the wait room. God also might move the teacher. Always approach God and ask for His will to be done. He may use experiences you consider negative to prepare you for greater service to His people here on earth. God is faithful to His servants. God knows when its best to keep exercising in the wait room and when it's time to move on.

God's Words of Encouragement

Many, O LORD my God, are the wonders You have done. The things You planned for us no one can recount to You; were I to speak and tell of them, they would be too many to declare. *Psalm 40:5*

When anxiety was great within me, Your consolation brought joy to my soul. *Psalm 94:19*

He has taken me to the banquet hall, and His banner over me is love. *Song of Songs 2:4*

[Jesus said,] "I will not leave you as orphans; I will come to you. Before long, the world will not see Me anymore, but you will see Me. Because I live, you also will live." *John 14:18–19*

May the God of hope fill you with all joy and peace as you trust in Him, so that you may overflow with hope by the power of the Holy Spirit. *Romans 15:13*

I know what it is to be in need, and I know what it is to have plenty. I have learned the secret of being content in any and every situation, whether well fed or hungry, whether living in plenty or in want. I can do everything through Him who gives me strength. *Philippians 4:12–13*

Those Wonderful Colleagues

My first teaching position was for all eight grades in a one-room schoolhouse. The congregation treated me with great kindness, but I soon missed having colleagues. That one-room schoolhouse was a lonely place after college classrooms and dorms with people stacked to the ceiling.

In my subsequent teaching positions, I discovered that colleagues bond into a family. When staff relations are good, colleagues become parents, brothers, and sisters. It's one group that will always accept you. The staff will affirm your strengths and abilities and offer support and forgiveness when you err. The group helps you control your pride and emotions, yet it provides you with an emotional release and gives you love and support when you're low.

Colleagues have the opportunity to minister to your needs immediately because of the unique work arrangement. Each day, God provides many openings to plant, to heal, to dream, and to pray for each other. At the Christian school, God's people work together. Here people don't just love you, they love you in Christ. Concern for one another becomes a way of life.

Colleagues give to each other in many ways. You give each other attention. It hurts to be unnoticed, ignored, or lonely. Attention from a colleague builds up your self-worth. You know the team cares. You also give each other understanding. Your colleagues know what it takes to get through the day, to prepare, to grade papers, to work long hours, to maintain discipline, and to help parents. Understanding may not always offer solutions, but it connects you as you work together to develop programs and learn new techniques.

Colleagues give each other encouragement. You offer help, urge each other on to better performance and success, and bring concerns and joys to God in prayer. Encouragement takes away misgivings and fears. Your colleagues really understand your needs, so the best encouragement comes from them.

Colleagues share the joy of being set apart for a special ministry. God joins you together to love and support one another. In such a family environment, it's easier to communicate love, encouragement, support, and faith to your students.

God's Words of Encouragement

Continue Your love to those who know You, Your righteousness to the upright in heart. *Psalm 36:10*

As iron sharpens iron, so one man sharpens another. *Proverbs 27:17*

I long to see you so that I may impart to you some spiritual gift to make you strong—that is, that you and I may be mutually encouraged by each other's faith. *Romans 1:11–12*

Love must be sincere. Hate what is evil; cling to what is good. Be devoted to one another in brotherly love. Honor one another above yourselves. Never be lacking in zeal, but keep your spiritual fervor, serving the Lord. Be joyful in hope, patient in affliction, faithful in prayer. Share with God's people who are in need. Practice hospitality. *Romans 12:9–13*

We always thank God for all of you, mentioning you in our prayers. We continually remember before our God and Father your work produced by faith, your labor prompted by love, and your endurance inspired by hope in our Lord Jesus Christ. *1 Thessalonians 1:2–3*

Your love has given me great joy and encouragement, because you, brother, have refreshed the hearts of the saints. *Philemon 1:7*

Show proper respect to everyone: Love the brotherhood of believers. *1 Peter 2:17*

*

Second Time Around

A month ago, the doctor had said that I was okay. I wasn't ready for this surprise. Now I was in the hospital, and with a life-threatening disease. I wasn't ready to give up my newly acquired retired status or the enjoyment of my two-and-a-half-year-old second marriage. As I spoke to God at this time of distress, my spirits were low. It's at times like this that God removes our confusion and shows us His love and His plans to restore us.

I belong to a congregation that truly ministers to its people. I know that God listened to many prayers on my behalf from this body of believers. The two church secretaries shared two Bible passages in their cards that I had often read. Now the passages offered new opportunities for reflection, a second pass to make a lasting impression.

The first passage was Deuteronomy 31:8:

The LORD Himself goes before you and will be with you; He will never leave you nor forsake you. Do not be afraid; do not be discouraged.

I had never looked at this passage when I felt that my life was threatened. I apologized to God for my fears. Why should I be afraid? God's promises answered all my doubts: He goes before me; He's with me; He won't leave me.

The second passage was 1 Corinthians 2:9:

No eye has seen, no ear has heard, no mind has conceived what God has prepared for those who love Him.

Those words grabbed my attention. I haven't seen or heard or been able to imagine what wonderful things God has, in His love, prepared for me. Whatever God has prepared for His dearly loved children is wonderful.

Time has shown me that some Scripture passages become special treasures because of our experiences. These passages get three stars in the margins of my Bible. I've also learned that the fellowship of believers that God places you in ministers to your many needs. Thank God for the friends He gives you in the body of Christ.

God's Words of Encouragement

Your consolation brought joy to my soul. *Psalm 94:19*

As the rain and the snow come down from heaven, and do not return to it without watering the earth and making it bud and flourish, ... so is My Word that goes out from My mouth: It will not return to Me empty, but will accomplish what I desire and achieve the purpose for which I sent it. *Isaiah 55:10–11*

[Jesus said,] "The words I have spoken to you are spirit and they are life." *John 6:63*

For God, who said, "Let light shine out of darkness," made His light shine in our hearts to give us the light of the knowledge of the glory of God in the face of Christ. *2 Corinthians 4:6*

Rejoice in the Lord always. I will say it again: Rejoice! Let your gentleness be evident to all. The Lord is near. Do not be anxious about anything, but in everything, by prayer and petition, with thanksgiving, present your requests to God. And the peace of God, which transcends all understanding, will guard your hearts and your minds in Christ Jesus. *Philippians 4:4–7*

And over all these virtues put on love, which binds them all together in perfect unity. Let the peace of Christ rule in your hearts, since as members of one body you were called to peace. And be thankful. *Colossians 3:14–15*

The word of God, … is at work in you who believe. *1 Thessalonians 2:13*

I Needed That

One time when I was feeling especially low, a colleague sent me a small box with a toy bird. The handwritten card read:

Faith is the bird that surmises the dawn—and sings while darkness still is there.

The bird and card took up residence on my file cabinet.

I needed that. I needed to see the plump little bird that seemed ready to burst into song because I didn't feel like singing. I needed those handwritten words to help me focus on the strength my faith in God could provide rather than on my miserable feelings and inadequacies. God already has a new day planned for me, and my faith hopes in it. Even while it's dark, I can learn to sing, trust, praise, and give thanks. I also needed to know someone cared. My colleague was sensitive to my feelings and took the time to show love and support.

A healthy Christian school staff is sensitive to each other's spiritual, emotional, and physical needs. Because teaching is strenuous, teachers need to support one another. Encouraging words provide a balm for any day, but especially a rough day. Let your colleagues know that you lift their needs to God in prayer and communicate your encouragement and support through words and deeds.

God's Words of Encouragement

Taste and see that the LORD is good; blessed is the man who takes refuge in Him. *Psalm 34:8*

Great is the LORD and most worthy of praise; His greatness no one can fathom. One generation will commend Your works to another; they will tell of Your mighty acts. *Psalm 145:3–4*

Seek the LORD while He may be found; call on Him while He is near. *Isaiah 55:6*

Therefore, since we have been justified through faith, we have peace with God through our Lord Jesus Christ, through whom we have gained access by faith into this grace in which we now stand. And we rejoice in the hope of the glory of God. Not only so, but we also rejoice in our sufferings, because we know that suffering produces perseverance; perseverance, character; and character, hope. And hope does not disappoint us, because God has poured out His love into our hearts by the Holy Spirit, whom He has given us. *Romans 5:1–5*

Set your minds on things above. *Colossians 3:2*

Are You Assertive?

Because teaching is a "people" profession, you soon become aware of how others, especially your students, respond to your leadership. One extreme finds students running the classroom. The other extreme is rigid, inflexible dominance by the teacher. Working at either end of the spectrum is neither professional nor will it accomplish much. Classrooms at either extreme exhibit little respect for self or for others.

As a successful teacher, you need to understand assertiveness. Assertive people avoid insults, blaming others, sarcasm, labeling, profanity, forceful language, or the belief that they're always right. Assertive people will exhibit honesty, give direct answers, and be open in all situations. Assertive people focus on the truth and identify realistic challenges. They celebrate their life with God and speak respectfully about themselves and others.

Most importantly, assertive people speak the truth in love. They admit to and apologize for any mistakes. Assertive people say yes or no graciously without feeling guilty about their response. They take responsibility for their decisions. Jesus was assertive. He obediently followed His Father's plan for the salvation of humanity. He willingly went to the cross to pay for our sins. Jesus gave His life to save the world because He knew it was His Father's will.

Assertiveness is not aggressiveness. Students should be allowed to assertively (respectfully, in love) ask you to

87

explain certain actions or choices. However, your students do not have the right to disobey you. You are obligated to discipline assertively, but you cannot be aggressively abusive. Aggression is really an attempt to play God. It exhibits a need to be right. Assertive people speak the truth in love, not in judgment. Wrongs and mistakes are honestly addressed, not to be destructive or vindictive, but to provide constructive advice for improvement.

God's Words of Encouragement

A gentle answer turns away wrath, but a harsh word stirs up anger. *Proverbs 15:1*

Speaking the truth in love, we will in all things grow up into Him who is the Head, that is, Christ. *Ephesians 4:15*

And this is my prayer: that your love may abound more and more in knowledge and depth and insight, so that you may be able to discern what is best and may be pure and blameless until the day of Christ, filled with the fruit of righteousness that comes through Jesus Christ—to the glory and praise of God. *Philippians 1:9–11*

The grace of our Lord was poured out on me abundantly, along with the faith and love that are in Christ Jesus. *1 Timothy 1:14*

I am not ashamed, because I know whom I have believed, and am convinced that He is able to guard what I have entrusted to Him for that day. What you heard from me, keep as the pattern of sound teaching, with faith and love in Christ Jesus. Guard the good deposit that was entrusted to you—guard it with the help of the Holy Spirit who lives in us. *2 Timothy 1:12–14*

Now that you have purified yourselves by obeying the truth so that you have sincere love for your brothers, love one another deeply, from the heart. For you have been born again, not of perishable seed, but of imperishable, through the living and enduring word of God. *1 Peter 1:22–23*

Above all, love each other deeply, because love covers over a multitude of sins. *1 Peter 4:8–11*

There is no fear in love. But perfect love drives out fear, because fear has to do with punishment. The one who fears is not made perfect in love. We love because He first loved us. *1 John 4:18–19*

Are You Meek?

In His Sermon on the Mount, Jesus says, "Blessed are the meek for they will inherit the earth." How can you be a teacher and be meek? The Bible says that Moses was meek. How can that be? He murdered an Egyptian and later led thousands of people for more than 40 years. We picture Jesus as being meek, yet He upset the money-changers' tables in the temple.

What are the characteristics of those who are meek? The meek do not use their positions for personal gain. They don't brag or try to impress others. They aren't self-imposing. The meek do not take on a false sense of importance, and they do not hold themselves above reproach.

In this pretentious world, those who are meek seem out of place when compared to the destructive, divisive personalities held up as role models. The meek choose to be assertive, but not in a defensive manner. They show inner strength because they back off rather than destroy relationships through self-serving attitudes.

True servants exhibit meekness. They aren't doormats, rather they speak honestly, and they lovingly try to accomplish their tasks. The meek have no need to impress others. They let God use their words and actions to accomplish His purposes.

God's Words of Encouragement

My eyes are ever on the LORD, for only He will release my feet from the snare. *Psalm 25:15*

A patient man has great understanding, but a quick-tempered man displays folly. *Proverbs 14:29*

I will leave within you the meek and humble, who trust in the name of the Lord. *Zephaniah 3:12*

I am not writing this to shame you, but to warn you, as my dear children. *1 Corinthians 4:14*

By the meekness and gentleness of Christ, I appeal to you. *2 Corinthians 10:1*

The goal of this command is love, which comes from a pure heart and a good conscience and a sincere faith. *1 Timothy 1:5*

All of you, clothe yourselves with humility toward one another, because "God opposes the proud but gives grace to the humble." Humble yourselves, therefore, under God's mighty hand, that He may lift you up in due time. *1 Peter 5:5–6*

Are You Spiritual?

Have you ever tried to develop a friendship, but somehow it never clicked? Sometimes our relationship with God seems like it's not clicking. We know about God. We can quote chapter and verse that describe what our relationship should be, but our *knowledge* of God doesn't make the relationship happen. We wonder what's missing. I knew someone who had been in church almost every Sunday, but on his deathbed, he wasn't sure of his relationship with God.

Psalm 66:16–20 says this about God's relationship with us:

> Come and listen, all you who fear God; let me tell you what He has done for me. I cried out to Him with my mouth; His praise was on my tongue. If I had cherished sin in my heart, the Lord would not have listened; but God has surely listened and heard my voice in prayer. Praise be to God, who has not rejected my prayer or withheld His love from me!

One important aspect of our relationship with God is confession. Psalm 66 says God will not listen to a heart that cherishes sin. We should daily confess our sins. Confession requires a deep regret that we have offended God. We pray in the words of the publican, "God, have mercy on me, a sinner." Confession touches the heart of our merciful God, and He responds to our pleas because Jesus suffered and died for our sins. God forgives us and restores our relationship with Him.

Psalm 66 also mentions our spiritual response of praise to God. God listens to those who thank and praise Him. Our praise and thanks completes the circle begun when God first touched our lives. He instilled faith through His Holy Spirit. This faith in turn frees us to obey God's commands. As we see God at work in our lives, we offer Him the thanks and praise due to Him as our almighty heavenly Father.

God's Words of Encouragement

Sing joyfully to the LORD, you righteous; it is fitting for the upright to praise Him. … Let all the earth fear the LORD; let all the people of the world revere Him. *Psalm 33:1, 8*

Call upon Me in the day of trouble; I will deliver you, and you will honor Me. *Psalm 50:15*

Save me from bloodguilt, O God, the God who saves me, and my tongue will sing of your righteousness. *Psalm 51:14*

My lips overflow with praise, for You teach me Your decrees. May my tongue sing of Your word, for all Your commands are righteous. May Your hand be ready to help me, for I have chosen Your precepts. I long for Your salvation, O LORD, and Your law is my delight. Let me live that I may praise You, and may Your laws sustain me. I have strayed like a lost sheep. Seek your servant, for I have not forgotten Your commands. *Psalm 119:171–176*

Offer yourselves to God, as those who have been brought from death to life. *Romans 6:13*

Never be lacking in zeal, but keep your spiritual fervor. *Romans 12:11*

We pray this so that the name of our Lord Jesus may be glorified in you, and you in Him. *2 Thessalonians 1:12*

When the kindness and love of God our Savior appeared, He saved us, not because of righteous things we had done, but because of His mercy. *Titus 3:4–5*

You also, like living stones, are being built into a spiritual house to be a holy priesthood. *1 Peter 2:5*

*

Encourage Students to Be Spiritual

The greatest challenge Christian teachers face is not teaching God's Word, rather it's encouraging students in their spiritual life. Students may attend Christian schools, but their general attitude, their language, and their relationships don't always reflect their faith.

Students live a spiritual life when they don't hinder the Holy Spirit's influence on their words and actions. Students not only need to know about God, but this relationship should motivate them to put into practice those things that God gives us to strengthen our faith. Encourage your students to confess their sins daily and take advantage of God's grace and forgiveness. Show your students the importance of prayer as a way to talk intimately with God and apprise Him of our needs and joys.

Christian teachers play a major role in encouraging their students' spiritual life. And students learn best when they observe your spirituality. Students are perceptive and cut quickly to the truth. Do your students know you love God? Do you daily display a personal relationship with your heavenly Father? Do you pray with your students in words they understand? Do you share God's Word with enthusiasm and choose passages that are appropriate for your students' age level? How do you react and respond to your students in the classroom?

Consider these ideas to help you encourage your students' spiritual lives.

1. Discuss what it means to live a spiritual life. Students

need to realize that just knowing who God is isn't living a spiritual life. Encourage them to ask God to send His Holy Spirit to guide their actions and words.

2. Help students identify ways to show their spirituality throughout the day—at recess, during class, and on the bus.

3. When students are in conflict, they should deal honestly with each other, confess any mistakes, forgive, and accept apologies.

4. Teach students what makes up a spiritual life: a respectful knowledge of God, confession, offering praise and thanksgiving to God, being aware of God's presence, and approaching God in prayer to seek His guidance.

Give students the opportunity to pray. You might play Christian music as your students sit and pray at their desks. Pass out a class list so they can pray for each other. Encourage them to make their own prayer lists. Remind them to pray for others as well as for themselves. Suggest specific types of prayers such as confession, intercession, and praise. Help the class make a collective prayer list on the chalkboard or a piece of poster board. Ask them to include prayers for community and world concerns.

Pray daily and fervently for the spirituality of your students. Approach God to help you encourage students in their relationships with Him. As a staff, pray often for your students' spiritual lives and include discussions of ways to encourage spirituality on meeting agendas.

Your spiritual life places God in the center of your personal life. Acknowledge and treasure His presence. Live a life of praise and thanks to God for His glory and saving acts. Our spiritual life celebrates our relationship with God.

God's Words of Encouragement

Blessed is the man who does not walk in the counsel of the wicked or stand in the way of sinners or sit in the seat of mockers. But his delight is in the law of the LORD, and on His law he meditates day and night. *Psalm 1:1–3*

May the words of my mouth and the meditation of my heart be pleasing in Your sight, O LORD, my Rock and my Redeemer. *Psalm 19:14*

Your word is a lamp to my feet and a light for my path. *Psalm 119:105*

Train a child in the way he should go, and when he is old he will not turn from it. *Proverbs 22:6*

We proclaim Him, admonishing and teaching everyone with all wisdom, so that we may present everyone perfect in Christ. To this end I labor, struggling with all His energy, which so powerfully works in me. *Colossians 1:28*

So then, just as you received Christ Jesus as Lord, continue to live in Him, rooted and built up in Him, strengthened in the faith as you were taught, and overflowing with thankfulness. *Colossians 2:6*

Preach the Word; be prepared in season and out of season; correct, rebuke, and encourage—with great patience and careful instruction. *2 Timothy 4:2*

But in your hearts set apart Christ as Lord. Always be prepared to give an answer to everyone who asks you to give the reason for the hope that you have. But do this with gentleness and respect. *1 Peter 3:15*

I have no greater joy than to hear that my children are walking in the truth. *3 John 1:4*

*

I Didn't Know Jesus
Till I Came Here

As you face your class for the first time, many unknowns confront you, including the spiritual status of your students. Some new enrollees may not know anything about Jesus. These students often blossom and burst into a vivid faith life. Here are some of my experiences sharing the Good News of Jesus with children who had never heard anything about Him.

Julia was a late arrival at our school. She didn't make or keep friends easily. She was overweight and suffered from poor self-esteem. And she was Jewish in a Christian school. Her mother was aware that her daughter would be taught about Jesus, but she felt that her daughter would remain true to the Jewish faith.

Julia loved class discussion and willingly participated. Toward the end of the year, she asked to stay after school, supposedly to help me. She really wanted to talk. Julia wanted to let me know that she believed in Jesus. I asked about her Jewish heritage. She said that she could have Jesus in her heart and still practice her Jewish faith. Julia and her mother moved before school even finished, but for part of that year, the door had opened.

Jon was a tall, lanky kid who attended our school for two years. At the end of the first year the teachers asked if he would return. Although Jon was smart and funny, he could be disruptive and often didn't complete his homework. Jon came back, and in the middle of that second year, he began to shape up. On the evening of graduation, he offered me his hand to say good-bye. Suddenly, Jon was in tears. As he gave me a big hug, he could barely get the words out to thank me. To him this Christian school had become something special. We had cared about him, and he wasn't coming back.

Eva enrolled as a seventh grader. She was a quiet, polite student, so it came as a surprise when we learned she was in trouble with drugs. After she was released from the rehab center, she stopped at school to explain how one of our morning devotions had helped her turn her life around. That devotion, which didn't stand out in my mind, had been the tool God used to change her life.

Brian came to our Christian school in the sixth grade because his mother was concerned with the music he liked. She called it satanic. We were never sure what Brian was thinking because he was reserved and his comments were brief. On graduation evening, he brought tears to my eyes with his statement about what Christian education meant to him. "I didn't know Jesus till I came here," he said, and then he proceeded to tell me what Jesus meant to him. Again, God opened the door for that one year Brian was with us.

We need to be just as concerned for students who come from Christian homes, those who have always attended Christian schools, children who claim the Christian faith. Often their lifestyles do not witness their faith in Jesus. We need to give students daily opportunities to learn about their Savior and put their faith into practice.

God's Words of Encouragement

For it is by grace you have been saved, through faith—and this not from yourselves, it is the gift of God—not by works, so that no one can boast. For we are God's workmanship, created in Christ Jesus to do good works, which God prepared in advance for us to do. *Ephesians 2:8–10*

Devote yourselves to prayer, being watchful and thankful. And pray for us, too, that God may open a door for our message, so that we may proclaim the mystery of Christ, for which I am in chains. Pray that I may proclaim it clearly, as I should. Be wise in the way you act toward outsiders; make the most of every opportunity. Let your conversation be always full of grace, seasoned with salt, so that you may know how to answer everyone. *Colossians 4:2–6*

Be faithful, even to the point of death, and I will give you the crown of life. *Revelation 2:10*

You Should Meet My Pastor

The relationship between a pastor and the teachers of a Christian school is vital. Negative criticism between coworkers disrupts their common ministry. The congregation where the pastor and the teaching staff have a good rapport is truly blessed. The entire staff can share, pray together, solve conflicts, and laugh together.

If you are in conflict with your pastor, take a look at yourself first. List the evidence that your feelings or comments are true. Pastors aren't perfect and their personalities do not always match your expectations. Ask God to help you resist the temptation to gossip about or sabotage your pastor. Discuss your problems with your pastor openly and honestly. Angry words and harsh criticism will only further destroy your relationship. Christians practice forgiveness. Make it part of your pastor-teacher relationship.

Pastors of congregations with Christian schools don't have easy ministries. Christian schools are costly ventures and may prevent other ministry ideas from being implemented, thus keeping pastors from pursuing new challenges. Pastors also must overcome preconceived notions that pastors and teachers should not get along. Pastors also may want to be involved with the staff and find it difficult to break into your clique. Take the initiative to be your pastor's friend. A pat on the back goes a long way for lifting each other's spirits. Both pastors and teachers need to provide avenues for friendship, caring, forgiveness, honesty, fun, and a shared sense of ministry.

101

God's Words of Encouragement

Seek peace and pursue it. *Psalm 34:14*

The words of a gossip are like choice morsels; they go down to a man's inmost parts. *Proverbs 26:22*

For as churning the milk produces butter, and as twisting the nose produces blood, so stirring up anger produces strife. *Proverbs 30:33*

I thank my God every time I remember you. In all my prayers for all of you, I always pray with joy because of your partnership in the gospel from the first day until now. *Philippians 1:3–5*

Therefore, as God's chosen people, holy and dearly loved, clothe yourselves with compassion, kindness, humility, gentleness and patience. Bear with each other and forgive whatever grievances you may have against one another. Forgive as the Lord forgave you. *Colossians 3:12–13*

May the Lord direct your hearts into God's love and Christ's perseverance. *2 Thessalonians 3:5*

But the wisdom that comes from heaven is first of all pure; then peace-loving, considerate, submissive, full of mercy and good fruit, impartial and sincere. Peacemakers who sow in peace raise a harvest of righteousness. *James 3:17–18*

All of you, live in harmony with one another; be sympathetic, love as brothers, be compassionate and humble. Do not repay evil with evil or insult with insult, but with blessing, because to this you were called so that you may inherit a blessing. *1 Peter 3:8–9*

Offer hospitality to one another. *1 Peter 4:9*

✻

Then There's My Principal

Happy is the school where teachers love and praise their principal. The structure of the staff can cause distance between the teachers and the principal. The principal as boss does not always place relationships in a positive context. It can be so easy to blame the person in charge.

No principal keeps everyone on the staff happy all the time. Differences of opinion are part of life. They add variety and challenge to daily living. Remember your principal was chosen for the position. Someone studied credentials, strengths, commitment, principles, abilities, and interests and employed your principal on the basis of those findings. Have confidence in this selection process.

Take a minute to really consider all that your principal's responsibilities entail. Your principal's decisions are constantly being held up for scrutiny. Even your actions reflect back on your principal.

Be positive in any discussions with your principal, even about negative situations. Pray for your principal, asking God to bless the management and leadership of your school. Be aware of your principal's activities so you can voice appreciation and support. Be assertive in your approach when you disagree, speaking the truth in love. Treat your principal as a friend, even if you sometimes disagree. Maintain an attitude of assistance rather than offering criticism without solutions.

Today's schools view the principal and teaching staff

as one team that generates ideas for running the school smoothly. This is a healthy attitude. Teachers contribute their professional knowledge and insights to give principals an "inside" look at the school. A good principal values this input and carefully considers any suggestions.

The teacher-principal relationship is a two-way street. As the school's leader, the principal has a serious obligation to teachers. As co-workers in the school, teachers have a serious obligation to their principal. The Christian school should take advantage of prayer to foster smooth relationships between principal and staff. Spend time in prayer during staff meetings. Meet for devotions each morning before your students arrive. When God is invited to direct and bless the actions of principal and staff, the door for harmony is opened wide.

God's Words of Encouragement

May the God who gives endurance and encouragement give you a spirit of unity among yourselves as you follow Christ Jesus, so that with one heart and mouth you may glorify the God and Father of our Lord Jesus Christ. *Romans 15:5–6*

Each of you should look not only to your own interests, but also to the interest of others. Your attitude should be the same as that of Christ Jesus: Who, being in the very nature of God, did not consider equality with God something to be grasped, but made Himself nothing, taking the very nature of a servant. *Philippians 2:4–7*

See to it that you complete the work you have received in the Lord. *Colossians 4:17*

Who is going to harm you if you are eager to do good? *1 Peter 3:13*

Where Do You Find Enough Time?

We live each day only once. If we waste any part of it because of poor planning or improper priorities, that time can never be recovered. Part of your responsibility as a teacher is to plan each day's activities for optimum learning.

You will be held accountable for meeting the demands of the yearly curriculum. Finishing only half the syllabus or text cheats your students. The days of the school year pass all too quickly, so pace your subject matter accordingly so that you will cover everything necessary.

If you are involved in activities that demand your time beyond scheduled class time, it becomes even more important to budget your time. If you are responsible for varsity sports, musicals, special religious services, clubs, or annual school activities, you might spend less time preparing for the next day. Don't be afraid to speak up at staff meetings if the extra-curricular activities keep you from performing your most important job—teaching.

God has priorities too. When Adam and Eve messed up and lost their perfect relationships with God, He made His salvation plan top priority. Nothing in the jumbled history of humanity sidetracked God from this goal. He constantly reminded the Israelites of the importance of telling the next generation about His ways. At the proper time, Jesus arrived on earth. During Jesus' life, He made ministry to people a priority. He rebuked the disciples when they thought little children weren't a priority. Jesus placed God's priority of salvation over His own desires and willingly went to the cross in our place. The Holy Spirit places top priority on calling, gathering, and enlightening people in the Christian faith. The world would be in trouble if the Holy Spirit chose another priority.

Life is full of choices, but not every choice carries the same value. Choosing the right or wrong priority can become a matter of life or death, of failing or succeeding. The Bible says, "Choose life so that you and your children may live." Ask God to guide your words and actions in the classroom to help you train your students to choose the right priorities in life.

God's Words of Encouragement

[Jesus said,] "If you are offering your gift at the altar and there remember that your brother has something against you, leave your gift there in front of the altar. First go and be reconciled to your brother; then come and offer your gift." (Priority: confession and forgiveness) *Matthew 5:23–24*

[Jesus said,] "Seek first His kingdom and His righteousness, and all these things will be given to you as well." (Priority: God) *Matthew 6:33*

[Jesus said,] "How can you say to your brother, 'Let me take the speck out of your eye.' when all the time there is a plank in your own eye? You hypocrite, first take the plank out of your own eye, and then you will see clearly to remove the speck from your brother's eye." (Priority: personal relationships) *Matthew 7:4–5*

[Jesus said,] "Let the little children come to Me, and do not hinder them, for the kingdom of God belongs to such as these." (Priority: children) *Mark 10:14*

[Jesus said,] "The gospel must first be preached to all nations." (Priority: preaching of the Gospel) *Mark 13.10*

*

Just Four Words

You woke up this morning with a dull headache. The class has been acting squirrelly all morning, and now Roger has had one of his outbursts. Your detailed schedule is way behind. You're ready to ask God for 10 minutes to talk the day over with Him, but there's no time. Math class should have started 10 minutes ago.

God is there in your classroom. He knows better than you how the day is going. At times like this, there's always enough time to whisper a four-word prayer: "God, bless my time." God hears these short prayers quite clearly. He knows you're asking Him to get you and your class back on track. He knows you want Him to be in charge of the day. God understands that you want Him to bless every moment of the day.

You usually look forward to the weekend. Most Friday nights, you and some of your colleagues get together for an evening of pizza and videos. But lately you never get very far with the video. Before you know it, the conversation turns to school. All of you are disgruntled, and you have become very supportive of each other as you pass the complaining blanket and the griping rag back and forth.

You're becoming increasingly disappointed with the way the evenings turn out and with the way you feel. You remember the professional high you were on at the beginning of the year, so determined to make this year successful. You have talked to teachers from other schools, but they seem to be coping with their problems without gossiping and backbiting. Turn the problem over to God with this four-word prayer: "God, bless my attitude." Whisper this prayer whenever your attitude gets bad or when you hear others pulling out the complaining blanket. God knows how important a good attitude is to your teaching ministry.

You need to talk to Roger, just like a thousand other times. He's having a bad day. His emotions, like yours, are out of control. Your heart fills with empathy. Whisper this four-word prayer as you walk to his desk: "God, bless my ministry." God loves Roger very much, and He will work through your ministry to bring change to Roger's life.

Prayer needs to be as big a part of your life as breathing. Trust that God will hear even the four-word prayers of a busy teacher. Daily seek guidance in God's Word and ask Him to bless your time, your attitude, and your ministry.

God's Words of Encouragement

Blessed are all who take refuge in Him. *Psalm 2:12*

In my distress I called to the LORD; I cried to my God for help. From His temple He heard my voice; my cry came before Him, into His ears. *Psalm 18:6*

The LORD is the strength of His people, a fortress of salvation for His anointed one. *Psalm 28:8*

Blessed is the man whose sin the LORD does not count against him and in whose spirit is no deceit. *Psalm 32:2*

Blessed are those whose strength is in You, who have set their hearts on pilgrimage. *Psalm 84:5*

Blessed are they whose ways are blameless, who walk according to the law of the LORD. Blessed are they who keep His statutes and seek Him with all their heart. *Psalm 119:1–2*

[God] fulfills the desires of those who fear Him; He hears their cry and saves them. *Psalm 145:19*

The LORD longs to be gracious to you; He rises to show you compassion. For the LORD is a God of justice. Blessed are all who wait for Him. *Isaiah 30:18*

Blessed are the pure in heart, for they will see God. *Matthew 5:8*

Blessed is the man who perseveres under trial. *James 1:12*

*

Don't Break a Child's Spirit

James Dobson wrote a book about breaking a child's willfulness without breaking the child's spirit. The following is a brief discussion of Dobson's main point.

A student acts willfully when he or she knows the rules and expectations and intentionally goes against them. An indicator of willfulness is repeatedly breaking the same rule despite your reminders and warnings. A student's spirit, on the other hand, is his or her zest for life. It makes a student active in positive ways.

When you discipline, the willfulness should be broken, not the student's spirit. Your disciplinary methods should hold the student responsible for those natural consequences of breaking the rule. Also, explain what is wrong and why. Continue to reinforce positive behaviors and clearly distinguish negative behaviors that require discipline. You might need to meet with the student's parents to explain your actions.

Be careful not to break the spirit of your willful student, which can be done easily if you respond in haste and without handling your own emotions. Never threaten or badger a student with discipline. Don't drag the student's problems to other teachers unless you want their advice. The student doesn't need a reputation that follows him or her for years. Give your student the chance to prove that he or she is under control. Offer honest praise whenever possible. Be friendly and show a positive attitude toward your student. The willful student needs your smile and time for conversation like all your other students—maybe even more so.

Don't give up on your willful student. Don't feel sorry for yourself either. View the student as your challenge. Your happiest moments in teaching will be when you have broken a student's willfulness and kept intact his or her healthy spirit for life. These are the students you will remember with pride.

God's Words of Encouragement

Keep your servant also from willful sins. *Psalm 19:13*

I will give them an undivided heart and put a new spirit in them. *Ezekiel 11:19*

[Jesus said,] "How often I have longed to gather your children together, ... but you were not willing." *Matthew 23:37*

And the child grew and became strong in spirit. *Luke 1:80*

And Jesus grew in wisdom and stature, and in favor with God and men. *Luke 2:52*

For I have not hesitated to proclaim to you the whole will of God. Keep watch over yourselves and all the flock of which the Holy Spirit has made you overseers. *Acts 20:27–28*

Carry each other's burdens, and in this way you will fulfill the law of Christ. *Galatians 6:2*

Therefore do not be foolish, but understand what the Lord's will is. *Ephesians 5:17*

Then make my joy complete by being like-minded, having the same love, being one in spirit and purpose. ... For it is God who works in you to will and to act according to His good purpose. *Philippians 2:2, 13*

God in My

CLASS-ROOM

Devotions for Christian Teachers

Ralph Beikmann

SAINT LOUIS